TSUNAMI
Housing and Problems

TSUNAMI
Housing and Problems

S. Surendran

Associate Professor and Head,
Department of Sociology,
South Travancore Hindu College,
Nagercoil, Kanyakumari District.

MJP Publishers

Chennai   New Delhi   Tirunelveli

ISBN 978-81-8094-209-9   **MJP Publishers**

All rights reserved   New No. 5 Muthu Kalathy Street,
Printed and bound in India   Triplicane,
Chennai 600 005

MJP 188   © Publishers, 2014

Publisher : J.C. Pillai

This book has been published in good faith that the work of the author is original. All efforts have been taken to make the material error-free. However, the author and publisher disclaim responsibility for any inadvertent errors.

Preface

The entire world was shocked when the giant waves of tsunami struck on 2004 along the coastal areas of India, and the countries of the east. The loss and havoc it created was irreparable and irreversible for years and the scar it has made will never fade from the land as well as the hearts of people. The giant waves washed away all that they could swallow along the seashores. Even huge skyscrapers were no exceptions. Nature was at its ferocious state that moment sparing none who came in front of it.

Aid from all over the world came flowing to help the victims in terms of food, clothing, basic needs, relief, rehabilitation and finally for counseling the ones who lost their dear ones and their belongings. Many international agencies came forward to provide housing for them. This book analyses the housing and living conditions of post tsunami in families in two villages – Mela Manakudy and Keela Manakudy of Kanyakumari district in Tamilnadu.

This analysis was based on the housing and living conditions on the 45 coastal villages in the district where 27 % were occupied in fishing. The people here had no knowledge of tsunami at all until it came and took their lives away. Their daily life was routine fishing and selling and thus making a livelihood. They included inland fishermen as well. Most of the fishing was by catamarans and mechanized boats. A pre and post tsunami comparison would definitely take us to the depth of the lives of these people where we can see how they are affected psychologically which would reflect on their lives.

This study was originally a research project pursued with a financial support of University Grants Commission (UGC). I record my sincere thanks to the UGC.

I owe my special gratitude to Er. P. Arumugam Pillai, Chairman, South Tranvancore Hindu College, Management, Nagercoil for his co-operative and cordial attitude through out my work.

I am immensely thankful to all the Board of Directors, South Travancore Hindu College, Nagercoil.

I am thankful to Dr.A. Meenakshi Sundarajan, (Former Principal), S.T. Hindu College, Mrs. Deepa Babu, Mr. John Bosco, Mrs. Benni Patriek (Assistant Prof. of Tamil, St. Johns Arts and Science College, Ammandivilai), Rev. Fr. Arulanthan, Priest, Meela Manakudy, Rev. Fr. Babu John, Keela Manakudy Rev. Fr. Dunston and others for their untiring co-operation.

Here I like to express my thanks to Mr. Panniadimai, Mr. Manoj, Miss. Sridha, Miss. Sugi for their co-operation in the field work and survey.

I am very thankful to the Respondents of Meela Manakudy and Keela Manakudy for their help from time to time.

In the end, I am thankful to all those as seen and unseen hands and heads who have been of way direct or indirect help in the embodiment and completion of this work.

I deem it my duty to express my deep sense of gratitude to my family and friends for their constant support throughout my career.

Dr. S. Surendran

Contents

Chapter 1

INTRODUCTION

INDIA AND ITS COASTLINE

India is a peninsular country. One-third of its land is surrounded with sea water. The main occupation which is done through water is fishing which plays a vital role in Indian economy.

India has its exclusive lengthy coastline of about 8118 km with a special economic zone of 2.02 million km², besides varied inland fisheries resources, comprising rivers, canals reservoirs, ponds, tanks, lakes, beaches and swamps besides brackish water area of 1.4 million hectares. Consecutively, India is the seventh largest fish producer in the world market. India has also been identified as the second largest inland fish producer.

FISHING INDUSTRY IN INDIA

Seven million people are directly or indirectly dependent on this fishing sector. The volume of sea food exported in the year 2000–2001 was worth Rs.6,309 crores. Fisheries sector has contributed Rs.22,223 crores to the gross domestic product in 1998–1999. India has an estimated overall fish production of 8.43 million tonnes with 3.9 million tonnes expected from marine fisheries. Based on the total production, India occupies third position in the world contributing little more 4 per cent to the world fish production.

About 1,00,000 fishing crafts ply along the country's extensive sea coast of which about 10,000 are mechanical boats and provide employment to about one million fishermen, the number of active fishermen being 25,000 and the number of marine fishing villages is about 1,800. Of the total persons employed, 67 per cent work on inland and coastal water fisheries while only 40 per cent of the inland waters are under culture

Fishery has provided employment directly for 3.08 lakh people whose livelihood depends on marine and inland waters. Besides direct employment, the industry is also an important income generator as it supports canneries and processing establishment; gear and equipment manufacturers, boat yards, refrigeration and ice-making plants and transport services.

India is there of protein production out of global output is placed at 4.3 per cent as against 15.3 per cent in the case of China, the leader in fish production. India's position continues at the same level which indicates the need of augmenting the fish production.

India has its locality in the tropical and subtropical belts which has its privilege of having ideally scripted agro-climate conditions for promoting the developmental activities at an extensive way. India ranks the first place among the common wealth countries.

Fishing industry in Tamil Nadu and Kanyakumari in particular

Tamil Nadu is one of the coastal states of India. The coastal length of Tamil Nadu is 1,000 km and the southwest coast is about 58 km long. There are 362 marine fishing landing centres in this area.

The contribution of fisheries to state domestic product was 1.1.25 per cent in the year 1995–1996 and it further increased to 1.841 per cent in 1999–2000. The share of fisheries income to primary sector was 5.398 per cent in the year 1995–1996 and it further increased 8.629 per cent in the year 1999–2000. This marginal increase has been mainly due to the higher growth rate of fisheries sector, a component of primary sector. The marine product exports of Tamil Nadu has increased as Rs.1,462.70 crore in the year 2000–2001.

Kanyakumari district is one of the significant districts of Tamil Nadu. It is located in the southern most tip of the Indian peninsula. This district is surrounded by sea waters. The sea coast extends from cape commission to Neerodi. There are 45 fishing landing centres. The fishermen have adopted their own traditional type of fishing methods. Their professional knowledge has its own unique features as fishing is the prime occupation of the people of this coastal district.

There are 44 marine fishing villages. There are 45 fishermen sangams in 28 coastal villages. There are five nationalised banks that cover the entire coastal villages of the district. The total population is 1,33,264 which contributes 27 per cent of the state's fishing population. Out of the total population, 48,306 are engaged in fishing activities. Non-governmental organizations are also engaged for fishermen's upliftment. The important organizations are the Kottar Social Service Society, the Kanyakumari District Fishermen Sangams Federation, the Santhidan and the Social Education for the Development.

These organizations have provided financial assistance, housing facilities and sanitation facilities. They also create awareness on social welfare and rights of the people. They have been liberating the fishermen from the clutches of local money lenders and also provide marking facilities in order to minimize the exploitation from the agents and middlemen. They have vested interest in the part of their future welfare. They have initiated the habit of saving money for future.

Both men and women in the coastal villages are equally contributing for the fishing industry, but men alone are engaged in catching fishes. They toil hard throughout the year yet their economic condition is poor and backward due to exploitation by middlemen and agents. Most of them are illiterates and are easily exploited. This leads to indebtedness and oppression. Their children are also forced to do the same occupation.

In 1997–1998 Kanyakumari district had 3,296 crafts out of which 2,683 were kattumaram and 613 plywood boats. This number increased insignificantly, that is, 759 trawlers, 186 gill-netter, 438 liner, 370 vallam and kattumaram 5,596 in 2000. These figures show that the number of kattumaram and vallam outnumber others among the total crafts of the district. The vallam and kattumaram are used by the fishermen traditionally. They are not in a position to switch over to new technique of fishing with big boats. The main reason is that they do have sufficient finance to invest. Even though nationalized banks are ready to provide financial assistance to invest in deep fishing, the fishermen are not interested to borrow loan from the banks. Another important reason is that they are not having repaying capacity.

A fisherman's income is not adequate to meet their daily needs and requirements. The family size of the fishermen is large in most of the cases while comparing their income level. The earners–dependents ratio of the family is very high. These people are involved in risky and dangerous occupation. They face number of accidents, storms and high tides may change their direction. At these times, they endure and starve for days together. Consequently, their family also starve. Some of the fishermen are behind the bars in jail in other countries for crossing the border. They have facilities for insurance, but due to their ignorance and lack of money, they have never come across such sources. Thus fishermen families with more number of children and less income cause suffering and that leads them to poverty.

Fishermen live in thatched huts in densely populated hamlets on the shore. They belong to the lowermost section of Tamil society and traditionally have to live outside the villages inhabited by the upper and middle class people. Fishing is the only source of income for these downtrodden and powerless people who constantly live under the threat of big-boat owners, moneylenders and merchants (Sridhar, 2005). Fishermen huts are located one behind the other or in a scattered manner to form a small settlement called "kuppam". They are very closely spaced in order to provide mutual shade to face the severe heat. Coconut mat walls facilitate airflow through the living areas to create a comfortable living space inside. These people were badly affected due to the tsunami. The population density in these fishing villages is almost three times higher than the average population density in the rest of the state (Krishna, 2005).

The need to live suitably close to the sea to enable fishing has resulted in most of them living in thatched huts, often very close to the shore. It was observed that the poorer fishermen live closer to the sea. The population density is striking in Kanyakumari where it is almost four times larger in the fishing villages than in the district.

The houses or buildings along the Kanyakumari coastal area generally consists of non-engineered and semi-engineered constructions, built with locally available materials like mud, coconut thatch, bricks, wood, etc. Typical fishermen huts consist of 1–3 rooms. It has small entrance with wide overhanging roof to face the severe climate, and consists of a living space and a semi-covered cooking space, the floor of which is finished with cow dung coating and mud to provide a cool and soothing environment inside. The thatched roof is often tied with coconut ropes. The houses belonging to rich families are made of bricks, finished with mud or cement mortar, and are covered with a tiled roof. Room sizes vary from 10 to 15 square meters. Another type of dwelling is a brick building with mud or cement and sand mortar. Pitched roofs are often covered with locally available mud tiles placed on wooden rafters. Majority of tsunami-hit areas consisted of rural houses, which were totally ravaged. Many reinforced cement concrete framed buildings faced partial collapse and non-structural damages.

The coastal area people do not have adequate sanitation and drinking water facilities. The magnitude of the challenge is underscored by the World Health Organization (WHO) estimates, ascribing about 80 per cent of all sicknesses and diseases to lack of safe water and sanitation, and evidence relating to higher incidence of communicable diseases such as diarrhoea, cholera, malaria, etc. in the country and indication of annual loss of 180 million man-days and Rs. 12 billion to the economy owing to sanitation-related diseases. The burden of diseases and lost livelihood opportunities has tremendous adverse effect on the life of the people in India in general, and in many cases, this has to be faced by the poor people living in the rural areas. The fishermen and women of the country are economically and socially weaker among the weak.

NATURAL DISASTER AND TSUNAMI

Natural disaster is one such a thing that threatens human race and gives a challenge to the modern scientific development. The tsunami in India on 26th December, 2004 is such a disaster which caused huge human and economic loss. This book tries to document the post-tsunami experience in India with special emphasis on Tamil Nadu.

Tsunami is a Japanese word which means "harbour wave". "tsu" means harbour and "nami" stands for wave. In general, tsunami means a large wave that is entirely different from the normal one, which is generated when the sea floor is deformed by seismic activity vertically displacing the over lying water in the ocean. Tsunami is a rare natural phenomenon consisting of a series of waves generated when a big lake or the sea is rapidly displaced on a massive scale. It can vary from unnoticeable change to devastation. The destruction of tsunami depends on its size and energy. If it is a big wave, it severely damages the coastal area in a massive manner; hence, it is called a killer wave.

Impact of Tsunami on Various Countries of the World

The impact of natural disaster (tsunami) on society and the environment are substantially larger in any country. Japan is the nation with the most recorded tsunami in the world. The earliest recorded disaster being that of the A.D. 684 Kakuho Earthquake. The number of tsunami in Japan totals 195 over a 1,313 year period, averaging one event every 6.7 years, the highest rate of occurrence in the world. These waves have hit with such violent fury that the entire town have been destroyed.

On December 26, 2004, an undersea earthquake measuring 9.3 on the Earthquake Magnitude scale has occurred 160 km (100 mi) off the western coast of Sumatra, Indonesia. It is the second largest earthquake in recorded history and generated massive tsunamis, which has caused widespread devastation when they hit land, leaving an estimated 230,000 people dead in countries around the Indian Ocean.

In 1607, Bristol Channel floods resulted in drowning of 2,000 or more people, houses and villages were swept away, farmland inundated and livestock destroyed, wrecking the local economy along the coasts of the Bristol Channel, UK. Some churches have plaques up to 8 ft above sea level to show how high the water rose.

The cause of the flood is not yet proven, but a research paper published in the journal Archaeology in the Severn Estuary [8] in 2002 following investigations by Professor Simon Haslett, from Bath Spa University, and Australian geologist Ted Bryant, from the University of Wollongong, proposed that the flooding was caused by a tsunami.

The British Geological Survey has suggested an earthquake on a known unstable fault off the coast of Ireland causing the vertical displacement of the sea floor as the possible cause.

1700 – VANCOUVER ISLAND, CANADA

January 26, 1700 - The Cascadia Earthquake, one of the largest earthquakes on record (estimated MW 9 magnitude), ruptured the Cascadia subduction zone (CSZ) offshore from Vancouver Island to northern California, and caused massive tsunami across the Pacific Northwest logged in Japan and oral traditions of the Native Americans. Brian F. Atwater, Musumi-Rokkaku Satoko, Satake Kenji, Tsuji Yoshinobu, Ueda Kazue, and David K. Yamaguch prepared a "scientific detective story" investigating this tsunami entitled The Orphan Tsunami of 1700— Japanese Clues to a Parent Earthquake in North America. This document is downloadable and available online.

1755 – LISBON, PORTUGAL

Ten thousand of Portuguese who survived the Great Lisbon Earthquake on November 1 were killed by a tsunami which followed a half an hour later. People fled to the waterfront, believing the area safe from fires and from falling debris from aftershocks. Before the great wall of water hit the harbour, water retreated, revealing lost cargo and forgotten shipwrecks. These people did not know that a Tsunami is a succession of waves, rather than just a single one.

The earthquake, tsunami, and many forest fires killed between 60,000 and 100,000 of Lisbon's re-quake population of 275,000. Historical records of explorations by Vasco da Gama and other early navigators were missing, and countless buildings were destroyed (including most examples of Portugal's Manueline architecture). Europeans of the 18th century struggled to understand the disaster within religious and rational belief systems. Philosophers of the Enlightenment, notably Voltaire, wrote about the event. The philosophical concept of the sublime, as described by philosopher Immanuel Kant in the Observations on the Feeling of the Beautiful and Sublime, took inspiration in part from attempts to comprehend the enormity of the Lisbon quake and tsunami.

The tsunami took just over 4 hours to travel over 1,000 miles to Cornwall in the United Kingdom. An account by Arnold Boscowitz (a century later) claimed "great loss of life."

1771 – YAEYAMA ISLANDS, OKINAWA, JAPAN

An undersea earthquake of estimated magnitude 7.4 occurred near Yaeyama Islands in Okinawa, Japan on 4 April 1771 at about 8 A.M. The earthquake is not believed to have directly resulted in any deaths, but a resulting tsunami is thought to have killed about 12,000 people, (9313 on the Yaeyama Islands and 2548 on Miyako Islands according to a source([9]). The seawater ran up on Ishigaki Island, ranges between 30 meters and 85.4 meters. The tsunami has abruptly stopped the growth of population in the islands, followed by malaria epidemics and crop failures which also reduced the population further. It was to be another 148 years before population returned to its pre-tsunami level.

1792 – TSUNAMI IN KYUSHU, JAPAN

Tsunamis were the main cause of death for Japan's worst-ever volcanic disaster, due to an eruption of Mount Unzen in Nagasaki Prefecture, Kyushu, Japan. It began towards the end of 1791 as a series of earthquakes on the western flank of Mount Unzen which gradually moved towards Fugen-dake, one of Mount Unzen's peaks. In February 1792, Fugen-dake started to erupt, triggering a lava flow which continued for two months.

Meanwhile, the earthquakes continued, shifting nearer to the city of Shimabara.

On the night of 21st May, two large earthquakes were followed by a collapse of the eastern flank of Mount Unzen's Mayuyama dome, causing an avalanche which swept through Shimabara and into Ariake Bay, triggering a tsunami. It is not known still whether the collapse occurred due to the eruption of the dome or of earthquakes. The tsunami struck Higo Province on the other side of Ariake Bay before bouncing back and hitting Shimabara again. Out of 15,000 fatalities around 5,000 thought to have been killed by the landslide, around 5,000 by the tsunami across the bay in Higo Province, and a further 5,000 by the tsunami returning to strike Shimabara.

1868 – HAWAIIAN ISLANDS LOCAL TSUNAMI GENERATED BY EARTHQUAKE

On April 2, 1868, a local earthquake with a magnitude estimated between 7.25 and 7.75 rocked the southeast coast of the Big Island of Hawaii. It triggered a landslide on the slopes of the Mauna Loa volcano, five miles north of Pahala, killing 31 people. A tsunami then claimed 46 additional lives. The villages of Punaluu, Ninole, Kawaa, Honuapo, and Keauhou Landing were severely damaged. According to one account, the tsunami "rolled in over the tops of the coconut trees, probably 60 feet high .... inland a distance of a quarter of a mile in some places, taking out to sea when it returned, houses, men, women, and almost everything movable." This was reported in the 1988 edition of Walter C. Dudley's book "Tsunami!" (ISBN 0-8248-1125-9).

1883 – KRAKATOA EXPLOSIVE ERUPTION

The island volcano of Krakatoa in Indonesia exploded with devastating fury on August 26-27, 1883, blowing its underground magma chamber partly empty so that much overlying land and seabed collapsed into it. A series of tsunami waves was generated from the collapse, some reaching a height of over 40 meters above sea level. Tsunami waves were observed throughout the Indian Ocean, the Pacific Ocean, the American West Coast, South America, and even as far away as the English Channel. On the facing coasts of Java and Sumatra the sea flood went many miles inland and caused such vast loss of life that one area was never resettled but went back to the jungle and is now the Ujung Kulon nature reserve. The aftermath of the tsunami that struck Newfoundland in 1929.

1896 – SANRIKU COAST, JAPAN

On 15 June 1896, at around 19:32 local time, a magnitude 8.5 undersea earthquake off the Sanriku coast of northeastern Honshu, Japan, triggered tsunami waves which struck the coast about half an hour later. Although the earthquake itself is not thought to have resulted in any fatalities, the waves, the highest recorded measurement of which reaching 38.2 meters, killed approximately 20,000 people.

1917 – HALIFAX EXPLOSION AND TSUNAMI

The Halifax Explosion occurred on Thursday, December 6, 1917 at 9:04:35 A.M. local time in Halifax, Nova Scotia in Canada, when the French munitions ship Mont-Blanc, bound for World War I France, collided with the Norwegian ship Imo, chartered to carry Belgian relief supplies. Mont-Blanc caught fire and exploded in the collision. The explosion caused a tsunami, and a pressure wave of air.

1923 – THE GREAT KANTO EARTHQUAKE, JAPAN

The Great Kanto Earthquake, which occurred in Eastern Japan on 1 September 1923, and devastated Tokyo, Yokohama and the surrounding areas, caused tsunami which struck the Shonan coast, Boso Peninsula, Izu Islands and the east coast of Izu Peninsula, within minutes in some cases. In Atami, waves reaching 12 meters were recorded. The tsunami damage include about 100 people killed along Yui-ga-hama beach in Kamakura and an estimated 50 people on the Enoshima causeway. However, tsunami only accounted for a small proportion of the final death toll of over 100,000, most of them were killed in fire.

1929 – NEWFOUNDLAND TSUNAMI

On November 18, 1929, an earthquake of magnitude 7.2 occurred beneath the Laurentian Slope on the Grand Banks. The earthquake was felt throughout the Atlantic Provinces of Canada and as far west as Ottawa and as far south as Claymont, Delaware.

The resulting tsunami measured over 7 meters in height and took about 2 hours to reach the Burin Peninsula on the south coast of Newfoundland, where 29 people lost their lives. It also snapped telegraph lines laid under the Atlantic.

1933 – SANRIKU COAST, JAPAN

On March 3, 1933, the Sanriku coast of northeastern Honshu, Japan which had already suffered a devastating tsunami in 1896 was again stuck by tsunami waves as a result of an off-shore magnitude 8.1 earthquake. The quake destroyed about 5,000 homes and killed 3,068 people, the vast majority as a result of tsunami waves. Especially hard hit was the coastal village of Taro (now part of Miyako city) in Iwate Prefecture, which lost 42% of its total population and 98% of its buildings. Taro is now protected by an enormous tsunami wall, currently 10 meters in height and over 2 kilometers long. The original wall, constructed in 1958, saved Taro from yet another destruction from the 1960 Chilean tsunami.

1944 – TONANKAI EARTHQUAKE, JAPAN

A magnitude 8.0 earthquake on 7 December 1944, about 20 km off the Shima Peninsula in Japan, which struck the Pacific coast of central Japan, mainly Mie, Aichi, and Shizuoka Prefectures. News of the event was downplayed by the authorities in order to protect wartime morale, and as a result the full extent of the damage was not known, but the quake was estimated to have killed 1223 people, the tsunami being the leading cause of the fatalities.

1946 – NANKAI EARTHQUAKE, JAPAN

The Nankai earthquake, a periodic earthquake of around magnitude 8.0 which occurs off the southern coast of Kii Peninsula and Shikoku, Japan every 100 to 150 years, last struck on *21* December 1946. The resulting tsunami hit the Pacific coast of western Japan. Particularly hard hit were the coastal towns of Kushimoto and Kainan on the Kii Peninsula. The quake led to more than 1400 deaths, tsunami being the leading cause .

1946 – PACIFIC TSUNAMI

Residents run from an approaching tsunami in Hilo, Hawai'i on April 1, Aleutian Island earthquake tsunami that killed 159 people on Hawai'i and five in Alaska (the lighthouse keepers at the Scotch Cap Light in the Aleutians) resulted in the creation of a tsunami warning system known as the Pacific Tsunami Warning System (specifically the PTWC), established in 1949 for Pacific Ocean area countries. The tsunami is known as the April Fools Day Tsunami in Hawai'i due to people thinking the warnings were an April Fools prank.

1958 – LITUYA BAY MEGATSUNAMI

On July 9, 1958, an earthquake with a magnitude of 8.3 on the Richter scale rocked a small inlet in Alaska called Lituya Bay. It then caused part of a mountain at the back of the bay to collapse, causing a monstrous tsunami to fly headlong through the bay. At a mountain at the mouth of the bay, the run was measured to be 524 m (about 1742 ft) making it the largest wave in recorded history. It swept three boats; one managed to ride the wave, but the other two were swept into the Pacific Ocean, where they were completely destroyed and four people on board were killed.

1960 – CHILEAN TSUNAMI

The magnitude 9.5 Great Chilean Earthquake of May 22, 1960 is the strongest earthquake ever recorded. Its epicentre, off the coast of South Central Chile, generated one of the most destructive tsunami of the 20th Century.

It spread across the entire Pacific Ocean, with waves measuring up to 25 meters high. The first tsunami arrived at Hilo approximately 14.8 hrs after it originated off the coast of South

Central Chile. The highest wave at Hilo Bay was measured at around 10.7 m (35 ft). 61 lives were lost allegedly due to people's failure to heed warning sirens.

Almost 22 hours after the quake, the waves hit the ill-fated Sanriku coast of Japan, reaching up to 3 m above high tide, and killed 142 people. Up to 6,000 people died in total world-wide due to the earthquake and tsunami. It brushed away three boats; one managed to ride the wave, but the other two were swept into the Pacific Ocean, where they completely destroyed and four people aboard were also killed.

1963 – VAJONT DAM MEGATSUNAMI

The Vajont Dam was completed in 1961 under Monte Toe, 100 km north of Venice, Italy. At 262 metres, it was one of the highest dams in the world. On October 9, 1963 an enormous landslide of about 260 million cubic metres of forest, earth, and rock, fell into the reservoir at up to 110 km per hour (68 mph). The resulting displacement of water caused 50 million cubic metres of water to overtop the dam in a 250-metre high wave. The flooding destroyed the villages of Longarone, Pirago, Rivalta, Villanova and Fae, killing 1,450 people. Almost 2,000 people (some sources report 1,909) perished in total.

The Vajont Dam as seen from Longarone today, showing approximately the top 60-70 metres of concrete. The 200-250 metre wall of water (megatsunami) that over-topped the dam would have obscured virtually all of the sky in this picture.

1964 – GOOD FRIDAY TSUNAMI

After the magnitude 8.6 "Good Friday Earthquake" tsunami struck Alaska, British Columbia, California, and coastal

Pacific Northwest towns, killing 121 people. The waves caused by the Tsunami were up to 23 m tall, and killed 11 people as far away as Crescent City, California. This happened on March 27, 1964

1976 – MORO GULF TSUNAMI

On August 16, 1976 at 12:11 A.M., a devastating earthquake of 7.9 hit the island of Mindanao, Philippines. It created a tsunami that devastated more than 700 km of coastline bordering Moro Gulf in the North Celebes Sea. An estimated number of victims for this tragedy left 5,000 dead, 2,200 missing or presumed dead, more than 9,500 people injured and a total of 93,500 people were left homeless. It devastated the cities of Cotabato, Pagadian, and Zamboanga, and the and provinces of Basilan, Lanao del Norte, Lanao del Sur, Maguindanao, Sultan Kudarat, Sulu, and Zamboanga del Sur.

1979 – TUMACO TSUNAMI

A magnitude 7.9 earthquake occurred on December 12, 1979 at 7:59:4.3 UTC along the Pacific coast of Colombia and Ecuador. The earthquake and the resulting tsunami caused the destruction of at least six fishing villages and the death of hundreds of people in the Colombian province of Narino. The earthquake was felt in Bogota, Cali, Popayan, Buenaventura, and several other cities and towns in Colombia and in Guayaquil, Esmeraldas, Quito, and other parts of Ecuador. When the Tumaco Tsunami hit the coast, it caused huge destruction in the city of Tumaco, as well as in the small towns of El Charco, San Juan, Mosquera, and Salahonda on the Pacific coast of Colombia. The total number of victims of this tragedy was 259 dead, 798 wounded and 95 missing or presumed dead.

1983 – SEA OF JAPAN TSUNAMI

On May 26, 1983 at 11:59:57 local time, a magnitude-7.7 earthquake occurred in the Sea of Japan, about 100 km west of the coast of Noshiro in Akita Prefecture, Japan. Out of the 107 fatalities, four were killed by the resulting tsunami, which struck communities along the coast, especially Aomori and Akita Prefectures and the east coast of Noto Peninsula. Footage of the tsunami hitting the fishing harbor of Wajima on Noto Peninsula was relayed on TV. The waves exceeded 10 meters in some areas. Three of the fatalities were along the east coast of South Korea (whether North Korea was affected is not known).

1993 – OKUSHIRI, HOKKAIDO TSUNAMI

Map of Hokkaido shown on NHK during an emergency broadcast. A devastating tsunami wave occurred along the coasts of Hokkaido in Japan as a result of a magnitude 7.8 earthquake, 80 miles offshore, on July 12, 1993.

Within minutes, the Japan Meteorological Agency issued a tsunami warning that screened on NHK in English and Japanese (archived at YouTube[10]). However, it was too late for Okushiri, a small island near the epicentre, struck with extremely big waves, some reaching 30 meters, within two to five minutes of the earthquake. Aonae, a village on a low-lying peninsula at the southern tip of the island, was devastated over the course of the following hour by 13 waves of over two meters' height arriving from multiple directions, including waves that had bounced back off Hokkaido—despite being surrounded by tsunami barriers. 250 people killed as a result of the quake, 197 were victims of the series of tsunamis that hit Okushiri; the waves also caused death on the coast of Hokkaido.

While many residents, remembering the 1983 tsunami, survived quickly evacuating on foot to higher ground, it is thought that many others underestimated how soon the waves would arrive (the 1983 tsunami took 17 minutes to hit Okushiri) and were killed as they attempted to evacuate by car along the village's narrow lanes. The highest wave of the tsunami was a staggering 31 meters (102 feet) high.

1998 – PAPUA NEW GUINEA

On 17 July 1998, a Papua New Guinea tsunami killed approximately 2200 people [11]. A 7.1 magnitude earthquake 24 km offshore was followed within 11 minutes by a tsunami about 12 m tall. While the magnitude of the quake was not large enough to create these waves directly, it is believed the earthquake generated an undersea landslide, which in turn caused the tsunami. The villages of Arop and Warapu were destroyed.

2004 – INDIAN OCEAN TSUNAMI

MAIN ARTICLE: 2004 INDIAN OCEAN EARTHQUAKE

The 2004 Indian Ocean earthquake; Tsunami strikes Ao Nang, Thailand. The 2004 Indian Ocean earthquake, which had a magnitude of 9.0 to 9.3,[12] triggered a series of lethal tsunami on December 26, 2004, that killed approximately 300,000 people (Including 168,000 in Indonesia alone), making it the deadliest tsunami as well as one of the deadliest natural disasters in the recorded history. It also had the second-largest earthquake in recorded history. The initial surge was measured at a height of approximately 108 feet, making it the largest earthquake-generated tsunami in recorded history. The tsunami killed people over an area ranging from the immediate vicinity of the quake in Indonesia, Thailand, and the north-western coast of Malaysia, to thousands of kilometres away in Bangladesh, India, Sri Lanka, the Maldives, and even as far away as Somalia, Kenya, and Tanzania. This is an example of a teletsunami which can travel vast , distances across the open ocean, in this case, it is an intercontinental tsunami. Tsunami waves 2.6 meters tall were reported even in places such as Mexico, nearly 13,000 km away from the epicentre. The energies for these waves travel along fault lines and becoming concentrated therefore travelling further. Unlike in the Pacific Ocean, there were no organized alert services covering the Indian Ocean. In light of the 2004 Indian Ocean tsunami, UNESCO and other world bodies have called for an international tsunami monitoring system.

2006 – SOUTH OF JAVA ISLAND TSUNAMI

MAIN ARTICLE: JULY 2006 JAVA EARTHQUAKE

A 7.7 magnitude earthquake rocked the Indian Ocean seabed on July 17, 2006, 200 km south of Pangandaran, a beautiful beach famous to surfers for its perfect waves. This earthquake triggered tsunami whose heights varied from 2 meters at Cilacap to 6 meters at Cimerak beach, where it swept away and flattened buildings as far as 400 meters away from the coastline. More than 800 people were reported missing or dead.

2006 – KURIL ISLANDS TSUNAMI

MAIN ARTICLE: 2006 KURIL ISLANDS TSUNAMI

On November 15, 2006, an 8.1 magnitude quake struck an area claimed by both Russia and Japan, but the waves near Japan did not swell up higher than 23 inches. There were no immediate reports of casualties or damage. Six hours later, tsunami waves up to nearly 5 feet high caused by the quake crashed into Crescent City, California and Santa Cruz, California causing considerable damages.

2007 - SOLOMON ISLANDS TSUNAMI

MAIN ARTICLE: 2007 SOLOMON ISLANDS EARTHQUAKE

On April 2, 2007, a powerful magnitude 8.1 (initially 7.6) earthquake hit the East- Pacific region about 25 miles (40 km) northwest of the Solomon Islands at 7:39 a.m., resulting in a tsunami that was up to 17 feet (5 meters) tall. The wave, which struck the coast of Solomon Islands (mainly Gizo), triggered region- wide tsunami warnings extended from Japan to New Zealand to Hawaii and the eastern seaboard of Australia. Dozens more have been injured with entire towns inundated by the sweeping water which travelled 300 meters inland in some places.

Simbo, Choiseul and Ranunga islands were also affected. A state of national emergency was declared for the Solomon Islands. On the island of Choiseul, a wall of water reported to be 30 feet high swept almost 400 meters inland destroying everything in its path. Officials estimate that the tsunami displaced more than 5000 residents all over the archipelago.

Impact of Tsunami on Tamil Nadu and in Particular on Kanyakumari

Natural calamities are not new to India; Tamil Nadu being located in a vulnerable part of peninsula region, the place is frequently subjected to devastation by cyclone, strong floods and drought. Tamil Nadu has faced seven severe cyclone and storms in the last decade. The cyclonic storms are more frequent in the Bay of Bengal than in the Arabian Sea. From the beginning of this century, 400 cyclonic storms have been formed in the Bay of Bengal whereas 80 storms in the Arabian Sea.

The 9.0 earthquake of the coast of northern Sumatra, Indonesia displaced a substantial amount of the sea bed, triggering a tsunami that struck the south eastern coast of India, as well as the Andaman and Nicobar Islands, at about 8.00 a.m. on Sunday, December 26, reaching up to ten metres high, the waves travelled as far as three kilometres inland. In India the water killed at least 12,405 people and approximately 5,640 are missing. About 8,000 deaths occurred in the state of Tamil Nadu, five districts bore the brunt of these losses – Chennai (250) Kancheepuram (250), Cuddalore (500), Kanyakumari (1,000) and Nagapattinam (6,000) deaths. At least one third of those who died in Nagapattinam were killed during services at Velankani Church – an important international pilgrim centre for Christians which is located within 200 meters of the shore. Most of those killed among them were women and children. Many fishermen lost their lives and belongings. The Tsunami has increased the number of widows by 63.1 percentage in the Nagapattinam district.

There are 13 coastal districts in Tamil Nadu with a coastal area of 1076 km, where 591 villages are situated. Kanyakumari is one among the coastal districts which is surrounded with three seas—Arabian Sea in the west, Bay of Bengal in the east and Indian Ocean in the southern side of the peninsular India.

The Tsunami that struck the Tamil Nadu coast as on 26th December, 2004 at about 10 a.m. astounded the whole world.

It is the greatest tragedy of the century for the nation. It was new to the loving memories of the coastal people of Kanyakumari district and this district is one of the worst hit areas. The coastal fishery is affected most in Kanyakumari district. Apart form the loss of human life among the fish folks, fishing boats and nets have been extensively damaged. The fishing harbours and the landing centres have also suffered heavy damage. The ecology of the coast is highly disturbed. The sea water incursion during the spring tide has further aggravated the ecological damages.

Tsunami had its impact on the following on a large scale:

- loss of human life,
- injuries to people,
- loss of habitat,
- loss of livelihood material,
- loss of infrastructure,
- ecological loss,
- heritage building loss, and
- the mental health.

The total marine fisherfolk population and their housing of the Kanyakumari district is 1,53,721 forming about 20% of fishermen of Tamilnadu. Though nearly 10,000 people lost their life in Tamilnadu coast, the mortality in Kanyakumari district is about 852. The death rate, loss of housing and properties are very high in places like Keezhamanakudi, Melamanakudi, Colochel, Kottilpadu, Azhikal, Muttum and Kadiaapattanam. Mortality rate shows severe sex differentiation in adults and children. In adult, of the total death, 23% were males, 30% female, 22% male children and 25 % female children, 47 %

children and 53% adults. Loss and damage to the houses are high in this district. 8304, 8123 and 15685 houses were within 500 meters from high tide limit. The following information indicates the houses damaged in the coast in each villages.

Table 1

Places	Numbers
Arokiapuram	117
Kanyakumari	0750
Vavuthurai	0103
Kovalam	1200
Kelamanakudi	1500
Melemanakudi	3000
Pallam	1135
Places	**Numbers**
Azikal	6500
Muttum	0600
Kadiapattinam	1200
colochel	5000
Rajakkamangalam	0185
Puthur	0300
Kottilpadu	0200

Source: Impact of Tsunami on Indian coast with special reference to Kanyakumari coast (R.S. Lal Mohan, Conservation of Nature Trust, Nagercoil, - 1, 2005).

Apart from houses, there were severe damages to crafts and gears and loss of infrastructure—damage of roads, bridges and waterways.

Effects of tsunami on the villages of Melamanakudi and Kelamanakudi

Tsunami has affected most of the coastal villages. Among the villages Melamanakudi and Kelamanakudi villages are considered as the hamlet of Thengamputhur revenue village, in Agatheeswaram taluk. Both the villages are situated in the west coast of Arabian Sea and on the western bank of the river Pazhayar. Melamanakudi and Kelamanakudi villages are village panchayats and administered by an elected panchayat President.

The villages Melamanakudi and Kelamanakudi are selected as the area of study. The total population of Melamanakudi is 4286 as per the latest census. Out of them 2174 are male and 2112 are female. Nearly 1885 persons are literate. There are nearly 1050 families living in this village. 350 families are living in Kelamanakudi. The total population is 2171, 1072 male and 1099 female. Most of the family members are engaged in occupation allied to fishing.

The fish folks mainly depend on sea for their livelihood and hence most of them have put up their houses nearby the seashore. Some of them have put up pucca houses. Many of the pucca and katcha houses on the seashore have been completely washed away and extensive damages caused to fishing boats and fishing accessories, and thus many of the fisher folks have lost their livelihood. The coastal economy has been paralyzed due to the loss of fishing gear and fisheries-related infrastructures.

The people of Melamanakudi and Kelamanakudi are doing hard work throughout the year but their economic conditions are very poor and they are still backward. They are socially open and deprived people even today. Most of fishermen are illiterates. The children are forced to do this occupation. Their family income is not sufficient to meet their requirement. They are involved in risky and dangerous occupations.

In Melamanakudi, the total death was 114. Out of them 39 are male and 75 are female. The age-wise death toll is furnished as below:

Age	Male	Female	Total
Up to 5 years	9	10	19
6 – 10 years	5	5	10
11–15 years	1	8	9
16 – 25 years	7	16	23
26 – 45 years	5	15	20
46 – 60 years	10	12	22
> 60 years	2	9	11
Total	39	75	114

18 women lost their husbands, became widows and 13 per cent became orphans due to the unprecedented tsunami. The Government of Tamil Nadu has estimated that the tsunami has damaged around 135,000 houses and invited humanitarian agencies to participate in the effort to rebuild an equivalent number of multihazard-resistant houses.

It has provided immediate visionary funds to the collectors to mobilize human and material resources for immediate relief and rescue operations. Roads and electricity supply has been restored within 72 hours.

Government has sanctioned relief to various categories of persons such as persons who lost their livelihood and sustained house damages, orphans, destitute widows, small traders, adolescent orphan girls, farmers, etc. The government also moved swiftly to provide temporary accommodation to the people who lost their houses by opening temporary relief camp in the following places:

1. St. Xavier's Church
2. Assisi Church

3. Carmel Nagar at Ramanputhoor

4. Lankadai Antony Church and

5. Nearby Schools

A cash compensation of Rs.8000 has been given to the victims who lost their livelihood, via District Collector through Thasildars and village officers after getting necessary acquaintance from them. Food and clothes has also been provided to the people through Government, NGOs, private sectors such as Lions Club, Swiss Karidhas, YMCA and kind-hearted public. Later cooking vessels, rice, kerosene and groceries, etc., were also supplied to them by the civil supply authorities of Kanyakumari District.

Melamanakudi tops the list of the villages where maximum number of houses got damaged. The damages caused in Melamanakudi village are listed below:

1.	Fully damaged houses	278
2.	Partly damaged houses	106
3.	St. Antheriyar Church	1
4.	St. Anthoniyar Church	1
5.	St. Thomayar Church	1
6.	Auditorium (Southern part)	1
7.	Bridge connecting Melamanakudi & Kela-manakudi	
8.	Primary Health Centre (Partly)	
9.	Palarpalli (Children School)	
10.	Graveyard	
11.	Fishing Industries	34
12.	Cable Connections	4
13.	Drinking water connections	
14.	Roads	2
15.	Vallam	81

16.	Fishing Nets	767
17.	Boat Engines	19
18.	Kattumaram	34
19.	Petty Shops	67

The cost of damage has been estimated as 245 lakhs.

Assessment of damages and losses incurred in Kela-manakudi village is listed hereunder:

1.	Fully damaged houses	187
2.	Partly damaged houses	170
3.	Thasnavis Matha Church	1
4.	The bridge connecting Melamanakudi & Kela-manakudi	
5.	Primary Health Centre (Partly)	
6.	Palarpalli (Children School)	
7.	Graveyard	
8.	Fishing nets	401
9.	Cable Connections	3
10.	Drinking water connections	
11.	Roads	2
12.	Vallam	21
13.	Fishing Nets	1500
14.	Boat Engines	
15.	Kattumaram	414
16.	Petty Shops	

Swiss Karidas made good of the church which was fully damaged. Swiss Karidas and KSSS-Kottar has adopted Mel-amanakudi village and has attended the relief measures of the worst affected village. The Swiss Karidas has also carried out the repair works of the library auditorium and partly damaged St. Antoniyar Primary School. They have supplied fishing nets and fishing equipments for restoring their regular work.

The Government have proposed to install an Early Warning System (EWS) in 30 coastal hamlets of Kanyakumari District through the collector. Steps are being taken by the collector of Kanyakumari to locate them in suitable places. One EWS is to be installed nearby Melamanakudi Panchayat office. The fishing folk feel this EWS will not protect them from the natural calamities like tsunami. During southwest monsoon there will be high tides in the seas, so the fishing folks are very much interested in building protective walls which would protect and help them in protecting from high tide and tsunami.

During the relief work, various social organisations constructed houses as a part of relief measures. The following table gives the information regarding the name of the social organisation and the number of houses constructed by them.

TATA company has constructed, 186 new houses, ROC – 183 houses, YMCA – 70 houses, CAC – 52 houses and Government 300 houses. The German Business Group and Sreenivasan Trust (sponsored by TVS Motors) constructed free medical check-up treatment hospital for the Kelamanakudi village people after tsunami incident.

The majority of the coastal villages affected by the tsunami have been 'adopted' for full reconstruction by NGOs, charity organisations, and private sector companies.

Role of NGOs/INGOs/Civil Society Organisations in Tsunami Relief and Rehabilitation

The degree of the disaster has been exceptional and the response to it is also extraordinary. Relief measures poured in from government and non-governmental organizations, religious organizations and corporate. The government of Tamil

Nadu, with assistance from the World Bank, the Asian Development Bank (ADB) and the UN Development Programme (UNDP) has developed a comprehensive Emergency Tsunami Reconstruction Project (ETRP). Under the ETRP, the government has planned to provide assistance to repair, rebuild or construct 140,000 damaged houses in Tamil Nadu and Pondicherry. (http://www.odihpn.org/report.asp?id=2798)

An NGO coordination centre has been established in Kanyakumari and a tsunami rehabilitation knowledge centre also designated by the district administration to oversee coordination of activities in this district. NGOs, voluntary organisations and public and private sector enterprises has been invited to 'adopt' villages for reconstruction, and freedom to choose their own architects and reconstruction approaches.

The role of NGOs can be looked at from various angles. In the immediate aftermath of the tsunami, the Tamil Nadu government took the lead in rescue and relief operations with the State Relief Commissioner's office working through the District Collectors. The government machinery was systematic and centralized. Cabinet ministers and senior officers of the Government were sent to the field to deal with rescue and relief. The NGOs has helped and their decentralized set-up has made response time quicker and also tuned to the community's immediate and actual requirements, NGOs has fulfilled the specific needs such as food, utensils or hygiene kits. Their need-based response really made relief faster. The relationships of NGOs with donor agencies meant that funds are quickly made available; similarly, some NGOs, because of their previous contacts and work with certain communities, were faster in identifying those left out and attended to their needs also.

Many NGOs have worked in the relief phase, setting up and/or repairing/refurbishing dozens of temporary shelters for those whose homes were destroyed as well as providing them with some components of support such as food, medical aid, water supply, etc. Some of them were faster in completing construction of permanent houses in the various districts as well as in providing medical and other support for the needy. Groups working with children set up child care centres and have supported orphaned children as well as those going to school with books and uniforms. They were also at the forefront in helping with trauma counselling.

Fishing communities were the most affected with the loss of boats and engines. Some of the NGOs had set up centres for repairing the boat and engine, manufacture of boats, ensuring high quality of work done in construction activities and livelihood restoration. NGOs had also worked for reclamation of salinated land in the tsunami affected areas paving the way for further packages of assistance from Government.

NGOs had made two-way information flow on the requirements of the villages and the materials available with the Government. During the first month of relief operations, they ensured a transparent relationship with the Government Officers on a daily basis, which then continued with regular meetings between the NGOs and other organizations with the District Administrations. Important corporates were also active in using innovative technologies such as the setting up of desalination plants to provide drinking water to the communities, repair of engines, desalination of salt affected lands, etc.

The Southern Region has played a significant role in all these efforts. In the rehabilitation phase, some of the NGOs have been promoting alternate technologies in building alternate livelihoods by conducting workshops and meetings to share expertise apart from their NGO coordination activities.

Shelter reconstruction is the largest ongoing activity in the rehabilitation phase. The Tamil Nadu government has decided on certain minimum requirements in terms of area of the house, ownership patterns, location and costs. With large number of organizations coming forward to construct houses, the Tamil Nadu government has decided to have formal MoUs (Memoranda of Understanding) with the organizations wanting to participate. NGOs are able to work closer with the community and rebuild according to the community's requirements and aspirations. Quality control and adherence to guidelines is likely to be stricter and accountability better, as these are relatively short term activities.

It appears a nearly ideal mix—the blending of the short term quick and appropriate response by the nongovernmental organizations coupled with the wider coverage and sustained activities by the government—in responding to a disaster of the magnitude of tsunami. It is also clear that coordination and information sharing is essential right from zero hour on to ensure that resources (both human and material) that are available are optimally used. Perhaps, the most important outcome of the tsunami disaster is the realization that governments and nongovernmental organizations can work successfully in partnership.

REHABILITATION

The relief phase is purely family-centred, providing basic day-to-day and immediate needs for the affected population. A breather to the tsunami affected in the form of temporary relief packages has served them confidence to live and strength to rebuild their lives. In order to quantify damage and do assessment sector by sector and to achieve the desired clarity on issues regarding reconstruction and resettlement, permanent housing, livelihood and infrastructure, the timeline and the content of rehabilitation, the state government held consultations with the beneficiaries, community leaders, local and district administrators, representatives from other states, NGO representatives and donor organizations.

Housing the homeless being the first priority, consultant engineers and other technical staff worked together with government officials in several workshops for detailing the guidelines for disaster reconstruction. It has aimed on precaution to be taken for construction, testing of materials, quality control, quality assurance, and other infrastructure like water supply, sanitation, road, rainwater harvesting, sanitary arrangements on construction site, construction of roads in rural areas and rigid pavement roads. It has been emphasized that the houses should be disaster-resistant.

To resettle the affected, the Tamil Nadu Government has formulated the housing policy under which permanent shelters will be built as per the Coastal Regulation Zone through MOU's between the District collectors and NGOs/Corporate undertaking construction of houses in the respective places. The state government has decided to give the newly constructed houses worth Rs.1,50,000/- with a built up area of 325 sq.ft, free of cost. Those people who are unwilling to shift beyond 200 m are allowed for repairing the authorized structures. Three cents of land in rural and 1.5 cents in municipal areas at free of cost.

New houses built are as per technical specifications of government for safety and durability. Insurance coverage would be given to the families for new houses for a period of 10 years. Legal ownership of the house is made in the joint name of husband and wife, or the survivor, or the eldest surviving child. Overall 89,206 permanent houses have been planned for reconstruction in the first phase across the state.

As on 22.12.2005, 5135 houses have been completed—1053 in Nagapattinam, 415 in Cuddalore, 981 houses in Kanyakumari, 468 in Thiruvallur and 2200 in Chennai. The design of these houses differ from place to place, according to soil condition and the desire of the people of that area (Page 262, Encyclopaedia of Disaster Management, Tsunami Disaster Managment, Volume 7, Arun Kumar Talwar and Satish Juneja, Commonwealth Publishers, New Delhi, 2008.) Relocation to the new house has given the fishermen families a new sense of safety, access to privileges that they never had and freedom from fear of being close to the sea.

The majority of NGOs have opted for full reconstruction by means of construction companies. The aim has been to replace all self-built traditional houses with 'modern' settlements of flat-roofed reinforced concrete buildings. The assumption that fishers live in independent nuclear families is also reflected in the design of the proposed houses, which have a standard size, divided into three or four rooms. None of the spaces is sufficiently large to allow an average family to stay together in one room. In general, houses have no veranda, or only a very small one. The new houses are constructed in rows on plots that are too small to allow for future additions. Where land can be found at an acceptable price, new villages are built on sites adjacent to the existing settlement. In most cases, however, no additional land can be found, and the new village is built on the same site as the old one.

Villagers are often forced to demolish their old houses and to surrender their land to make space for the construction of the new village. The social tensions emerging out of these processes are already tangible, as families whose houses were not damaged by the tsunami try to resist demolition. Many companies require completely clear ground before starting construction, necessitating removing all trees. It is hard to imagine how people would live in a tiny flat-roofed cement houses without any shade where the temperature typically reach 40 degrees centigrade.

Construction companies have a tendency to build standard houses that do not meet the specific requirements of the families for whom they are intended. When construction materials and expertise are imported from outside, communities may find it difficult to repair or maintain their new homes. Villages reconstructed houses are generally consist of grid-patterned row houses that pay little attention to communities' social organisation and settlement patterns. It is also analysed that Post-disaster housing and resettlement schemes often lead to social dislocation and a breakdown of informal social security systems. Occupancy rates for houses constructed by external agencies often remain low, as people refuse to move in.

Significance of Challenges in Tsunami Housing Programmes

This book signifies certain challenges in the Tsunami housing programmes, both for the private organisations and the government. Firstly, the construction of houses has been distributed to a large number of organisations, which has made the progress slow. To date only 50 per cent of the houses have been completed. Secondly, the government has faced the dilemma of ensuring that the people are not displaced to places far away from their earlier habitat and livelihood. There are difficulties in acquisition of land as the required size of site is often large and in several instances, land is not suitable for construction of houses. Thirdly, there have been delays in provision of basic infrastructure, such as electricity, water, sanitation and roads. The houses that are handed over to the beneficiaries do not have even basic infrastructure in place. Fourthly, there have been limitations in monitoring construction, leading to poor quality housing in some of the sites, in terms of material used, designs, construction methods, and techniques. Fifthly, with few positive exceptions, the approach has been provision of houses, rather than developing habitats. The housing programme would have benefited from a more holistic approach, if the various dimensions of housing such as community infrastructure, water, sanitation, environment and conservation and livelihood had been addressed in a more integrated and timely manner. Indeed in several sites, it has been observed that houses were handed over to beneficiaries without infrastructure and services readily available.

The focus of this book is on housing and living conditions of post-tsunami families in Kelamanakudi and Melamanakudi villages of Kanyakumari district in 2010 within the framework.

The present chapter serves as an introduction that has presented a clear scenario of coastal livelihood of Kanyakumari district. It also presents the housing and habitat development approach and also addresses the interrelated issues pertaining to housing, sustainable livelihood, environment, and conservation of the people belonging to the villages Mela- manakudi and Kelamanakudi.

The second chapter crucially reflects the impact of tsunami in India and in other countries and recovery efforts carried over in India over the last six years and also depicts the livelihood and occupation of the fishermen community. It also elucidates the present scenario of several researchers in the analysis of tsunami.

The third chapter is the arrangement of conditions for collection and analysis of information.

The fourth chapter aims to provide a clear information on achievements and the problems focused in each of the sectors: housing, water and sanitation, pre- and post-tsunami livelihoods and assets, environment, reliefs, psychosocial care & counselling, satisfaction of housing facilities, and support for women and children have been clearly interpreted.

The final chapter focuses on the the post-tsunami housing and living conditions and suitable suggestions for their improvment.

Chapter 2

TSUNAMI—LOST LANDS

This chapter provides a comprehensive overview of tsunami and its impact in various places, the destruction, the damages and the measures and cumulative achievements in relief and recovery efforts thereon. Six years have passed since the tsunami, triggered by the massive earthquake off the coast of Sumatra, struck the Indian coast. The tsunami recovery work is still in full swing.

DEVASTATING EFFECT OF TSUNAMI IN INDIA AND OTHER FOREIGN COUNTRIES

In history, there are a lot of evidences for the occurrence of tsunami in many regions including Poompuhar (Tamilnadu, India) in Circa 500 BC. On January 26, 1700 the Cascadia earthquake (estimated at 9 Richter scale magnitudes) caused massive tsunami across the Pacific Northwest. In 1896, one of the worst tsunami disasters engulfed whole villages along Sanrikym (Japan) and drowned some 26,000 people. In 1946, an earthquake in the Aleutian Islands sent a tsunami to Hawaii, killing 159 people. On July 9, 1958, a huge landslip caused a tsunami in the Fjord shaped Lituya Bay, Alaska, USA; it travelled at over 150 km/h. On May 26, 1983, 104 people in

Western Japan were killed by a tsunami spawned from a nearby earthquake. In July 1998, a Papua New Guinea tsunami killed approximately 2,200 people. It was a 7.1 magnitude earthquake; 24 km offshore was swallowed within 11 minutes by the tsunami wave about 12 m tall.

In spite of the historical recurrence, many in India were unaware of term tsunami till December 26, 2004. On December 26, 2004 tsunami shook the entire world and was recorded as a black day in the human history. It was an undersea earthquake that occurred at 8 a.m. mainly in Sumatra Island in Indonesia and Andaman & Nicobar Islands in India in the Indian Ocean. The magnitude of the earthquake was recorded as 9.3 in Richter scale. At this magnitude, since 1900, it is the second largest earthquake ever recorded on a seismograph. The previous earthquake in the year 1960 (Great Chilean Earthquake) recorded with a greater magnitude of 9.5 Richter scale. The present earthquake triggered a series of lethal tsunamis that spread through out the Indian Ocean, killing large number of people and devastating coastal communities across South and South East Asia, including parts of Indonesia, Sri Lanka, India, Thailand and elsewhere. It was estimated that there were 1,84,168 casualties and 42,883 persons missing, and a total of 2,20,866 persons were affected. Indonesia was the worst affected country with a human toll of 1,30,736 which is far more than 70 per cent in the total tsunami deaths recorded in all the affected countries. Indonesia was followed by Sri Lanka, India and Thailand.[1]

The devastation caused by the Tsunami on 26th December 2004, has left coastal lands flattened and billions of dollars worth infrastructure, economic assets and materials were devastated. It had severe impact on coastal fishing communities in Tamil Nadu destroying houses, boats, fishing gear, agricultural land and salt-pans wiping out the livelihoods of millions of people.

The fishermen community are identified as social group because they are engaged with a particular occupation and most of them belong to a particular religion. They are tied with a sense of unity. The financial conditions and their livelihood of the fishermen are deprived. The perspectives of various researchers are as follows:

Sankaran Pillai C and **J.K Stephen**, revealed that the economic conditions of fishermen was very poor and their community was backward. The economic and rural backwardness of the fishermen is nothing but an outcome of their unskilled and non-migratory nature. They are not capable of doing any manual work other than fishing. They are not tried to implement modern techniques of fishing. Hence their income seldom goes beyond their subsistence level.

Pitchiah N (1987) revealed that the fishermen community suffered from economic backwardness. They are exploited by the middlemen and ultimately suffered with poverty. They suffered in poverty as they had not taken a family planning. They are continuing outdated techniques of fishing. As a result their income earning is very low.

Sentilathiban R.C and **Selvaraj (1987)** revealed that fishing households are traditionally low in status, live in poor economic conditions and they are fishing labourers.

Sridevi S (1989) pointed out that a large number of fishermen are not able to meet the basic needs of their families and hence the women members of the families are forced to make their entry into the fishing industry.

Selvaraj C (1975) revealed that catamarans are poor and inadequate to maintain the small fishing families even at the subsistence level. There is a wide divergence between motor boat owners and catamaran fishermen in respect of their income.

Apart from the subsidy amount that was given to the fishermen by the Government of Tamil Nadu, as a long-term measure, linkage was given by the government between the fishermen and the banks for loans to the tune of Rs.47 cores to about 2000 fishermen for repairing/replacing their fishing craft. The state government has exempted fishing gear from sales tax. 8 ports, 15 fishing harbours and innumerable fish landing centres are being restored. Besides supporting the fishing implements, they need to be given psychological strength to dare the sea again.

In Tamil Nadu there are 595 fishing villages and 362 fish landing centres spread over 13 coastal districts with 1,45,000 fisher households. About 2.85 lakhs marine fishers are actively engaged in fishing in the coastal water of Tamil Nadu.

Tamil Nadu is one of the major exporter of marine products in the country exporting marine products to the tune of 70147m. tons are realizing a value of Rs.25 billion. The share of this state in total quantity of fish exported is 36.44 percentage.

The fishers in Tamil Nadu in 2002–2003, the latest year for which data are available, produced about 15 per cent of the state's fish exports, which accounted for 36.5 per cent of the value of all fishing products exported from India. Most adult males (87 per cent in 2002–2003) are employed exclusively in fishing activities, while women are primarily responsible for marketing of fresh and dried fish.

NGO representatives reported group-bonded labourers (fishermen coolies) who work for other fishermen in their own villages despite their being of the same caste. These labourers, mostly in the southern parts of Tamil Nadu, receive advance from boat owners in exchange for an agreement to work on the employer's boats. Crews are comprised of four to five bonded labourers, who usually receive one-third of the harvest at the end of the day to divide amongst themselves and receive a daily wage of Rs.80–100 (US $1.83–2.29) per day. From their earnings, the bonded labourers must repay their initial advance. Given the meagre earnings, the labourers in practice find it difficult if not impossible to satisfy their debt and leave their employers.

The tsunami that hit Coromandel coast of India on that day was caused by a massive earthquake on the Indian Ocean near Sumatra in Indonesia. Similar waves have hit six other countries, claiming thousands of lives. Tamil Nadu was one of the worst affected due to tsunami.

Several coastal districts of Tamil Nadu that bore the brunt of the devastating tidal waves are listed:

Government Informanation Cell Reveneue Administration Disaster Management and Mitigation Department Damages (As on 20th January 2005 at 10:00 Hrs. IST)

Sl.No	Districts affected	No. of Villages / Kuppams affected	Population affected	Houses / Huts Damaged	No. of Human Lives Lost	No. of injured
1.	Chennai	24	65322	17805	206	9
2.	Kancheepuram	44	100000	7043	128	11
3.	Thiruvallur	6	15600	4147	29	0
4.	Cuddalore	51	99704	15200	617	214
5.	Villupuram	33	78240	9500	47	30
6.	Nagapattinam	73	196184	36860	6063	1922
7.	Tiruvarur	0	0	0	21	0
8.	Thanjavur	22	29278	3	30	421
9.	Kanyakumari	33	187650	31175	824	525
10.	Thoothukudi	23	30505	735	3	0
11.	Tirunelveli	10	27948	630	4	4
12.	Ramanathapuram	0	0	6	6	0
13.	Puthukottai	25	66350	1	15	0
Total		345	896781	123105	7993	3136

STUDY OF THE DAMAGE CAUSED BY TSUNAMI IN KANYAKUMARI

The total length of Kanyakumari coastline is 67 km and there are 44 villages located in this coastal belt. The entire rows of houses along the seashore have been washed away. The small harbour where the fishing boats had been tied were completely destroyed, especially in Melamanakudy and Kelamanakudy villages. The safety walls are scattered to smithereens. The bridge built at Manakudi just before 2 years has been thrown 300 meters away from its location. This was the bridge connecting Kanyakumari–Trivandrum Coastal Highway cutting the distance by 32 km.

Property Damages at Melemanakudy

- The houses damaged are .... nos
- The reported number of boats lost is ..... (data from the Diocese)
- The reported number of Vallams lost is   (data from the Diocese)

- The reported number of Cattamaram lost is
- The reported number of nets lost is

The roads are ruined. Bridges have collapsed. Electric poles are uprooted. Telephone lines are cut. Water pipes are broken. Salt water has entered the low lying area and increased the PHC concentration considerably. Drinking water has been polluted.

Four wheelers had been carried into the sea or mangled completely. Almost all two wheelers in the affected areas are smashed and can be used no longer. The loss of golden ornaments is huge. No household articles from the damaged houses can be used. People have lost kitchen utensils, vessels, groceries and grains, TV, music system and much more. Children have lost all their books, note books and study materials. What is worse, the people are greatly traumatised, an indelible scar has maimed them; they are greatly scared and nearly lost hope.

INFORMATION ON THE COASTAL LAND OF THE DISTRICT

List of Coastal Villages

1.	Arockiyapuram	22.	Periya Villai
2.	Chinna Muttom	23.	Puthoor
3.	Kanyakumari	24.	Kottil Padu
4.	Vavathurai	25.	Maramady
5.	Puthugramam	26.	Simon Colony
6.	Siluvai Nagar	27.	Kodimunai
7.	Kovalam	28.	Vania Kudy
8.	Kelamanakudi	29.	Kurumpanai
9.	Melamanakudi	30.	Helen Colony
10.	Annai Nagar	31.	Enayam
11.	Pallam	32.	Enayam Puthanthurai
12.	Puthan Thurai	33.	Raman Thurai
13.	Kesavan Puthanthurai	34.	Mullor Thurai
14.	Pozhikarai	35.	Poothurai
15.	Peria Kadu	36.	Erayaman Thurai
16.	Rajakamangalam Thurai	37.	Thoothoor
17.	Azhikal	38.	Thoothoor Chinna Thurai
18.	Pillaithoppu	39.	Eraviputhan Thurai
19.	Muttam	40.	Vallavillai
20.	James Nagar	41.	Neerody
21.	Kadiyapattinam	42.	Marthandam Thurai

In Kanyakumari district 10407 catamarans were fully damaged and 264 were party damaged. 2428 vallams were fully damaged and 857 vallams were partly damaged, 505 mechanised boats were fully damaged and 346 were partly damaged.

69.65 million ton nets were damaged and 90 engines were damaged.

Demography and Fishing Crafts – (SIFFS – February 2003)

Total population	1,38,569
Total houses	31,595
No. of boats already registered	1,379
No.of kattumaram	6,053
Vallams	1,747

Fishing Nets

Kachavalai	2236
Chazhavalai	2050
Discovalai	3080
Vazhuvalai	1175
Echavalai	628
Thathuvalai	733
Kal Ral Valai	659
Iluvalai	530
Otha Kundu Valai	519
Vazha Valai	301
Valacha Valai	5

Manangu Valai	125
Vaval Valai	75
Thiruka Valai	38
Paduka Meen Valai	211
Thattumadi	296
Karamadi	280
Total	12,365

RELIEF AND REHABILITATION MEASURES UNDERTAKEN BY GOVERNMENT AND NGO'S

Food Supply and Medical Relief

Soon after tsunami, 76 relief camps were established. Later, 26 relief camps were also established in addition for the accommodation of 68,647 victims. Basic needs such as food, shelter and clothing were provided in the relief camps. Volunteers took the injured and fractured persons to the hospital for treatment. A team of doctors were involved in providing medical assistance to the people suffering with the support of CHDP team. They visited camps and provided their assistance to the sick. All required preventive and curative medicines were supplied by KSSS. KSSS took much effort for the well being of the volunteers by providing them with vaccination, etc.

People in the temporary Relief Camps needed proper supply of food. Sanitation was a major problem in the camps. KSSS and Diocesan Machinery with the support of local parishioners made all possible arrangements for their stay in the camps. The KSSS team monitored every camp with the support of NGOs and the Government Departments. KSSS extended its financial assistance to the construction of few temporary shelters apart from shelters put up by the government. Financial assistance was given to the construction of bathrooms, toilets, washing points and bore wells.

In Melamanakudy and Kelamanakudy villages the total number of food kit distributed by the KSSS was 1,050. It also supplied nutritious food for pregnant women and children. It also supplied sanitary napkins and garments to women. They supplied uniforms and study materials to the school students.

KSSS organised a networking of all the NGO functioning in the disaster area. 27 NGOs came under the networking and divided the work among themselves. KSSS took the role of the convener. Many INGOs also came to the area with various resources. KSSS organized these INGOs and formed a forum called "Kanyakumari District Tsunami Relief and Rehabilitation forum" in order to plan and execute relief and rehabilitation work in the affected areas. Each INGOs was entrusted with a set of villages for undertaking rehabilitation work. To reach out to the victims of tsunami, coordination, relief work, finance, counselling, advocacy with government, Documentation, Health Care, Information, and media committees were formed. Each committee made an elaborate arrangement with the support of volunteers and staff and accomplished a meaningful and committed service in the respective areas allotted to them.

Water Supply

The water sources in Melamanakudy and Kelamanakudy villages were fully damaged due to tsunami waves. The initial step was assisted cleaning and repairing open wells in these villages.

A technical team cleaned the wells and a new side wall was built. The platform of the well with amenities was used to draw water with proper drainage system near the open well. These arrangements have paved way for the cleanliness and better hygiene in the surrounding areas. Over 400 families benefited from these five open wells.

Rehabilitation Assistance

In Melamanakudi village a tailoring institute was started and 42 girls and poor ladies are learning. 57 cents of land has been brought at Sinclairpuri to establish tsunami rehabilitation projects beginning with fashion technology as well as computer training institute.

Nanjii Natham, the official TV media of the Diocese telecasted helpline phones, phone numbers to be contacted in relief camps and persons to be contacted for various purposes. Nanjil Natham telecasted the magnitude of the devastation and announced the needs of the tsunami victims periodically and the relief work undertaken by the Diocese & KSSS.

Having seen the agony and pain of the Tsunami victims, Bishop of Kottar invited religious leaders of other faith and political leaders to plan the relief activities for the victims of Tsunami. Many religious and political leaders took part in the meeting to express their solidarity in addressing the needs of tsunami victims. Consequently the party members and religious leaders submitted a memorandum to the District collector demanding the government to take appropriate measures to help the victims.

All the affected families were provided with one net each, out of the six different types of nets fishermen commonly use during various seasons, with the help of friendly agencies, bought with the assistance of Caritas Austria/Diocese of Voralberg.

They have to brace over so often with the vagaries of the weather, natural calamities and the rough waves. Their future remains bleak; uncertainty and insecurity of life drives them to live for now; they have practically no saving and alcoholism is one solace for all trouble in the coastal belt. Church activities are given a pride of place in their day-to-day life. Through own fishing boats, most of them have had just the Catamaram. Since the government has restricted the use of motorised Vallam, they use detachable engines.

Setting Up of Orphanages by NGO's

Many of the children and the aged were wounded or injured when they ran for safety when the waves struck. In some villages, the number of children killed by the tsunami was higher than the number of men killed. At the same time, over 350 children in Tamil Nadu were orphaned by the tsunami. In response, the state government of Tamil Nadu has created a fund for tsunami orphans and has created bank account in the name of each orphan. Each account has Rs.500000 (US$ 11,700), which the beneficiary may cash only upon reaching eighteen years of age. In addition, the government has built orphanages for tsunami orphans in affected districts. However, some of the children have refused to enter these orphanages because they do not wish to move away from their own villages. In these cases, relatives and neighbours have taken them in, a few NGOs have began to support orphans living with relatives with monthly cash payments; other groups plan to open orphanages for the children in their own villages so that they may remain in the community.

Construction of Disaster-resistant Houses

Housing has been the most affected sector next to fisheries due to tsunami of 26 December 2004. Three districts namely Nagapattinam, Kanyakumari and Cuddalore were the worst affected districts. Preliminary survey indicated that in rural areas 90,000 houses need to be reconstructed and 10,000 houses need to be repaired. In urban areas 31,300 houses were expected to be reconstructed and 1107 houses needed to be repaired.

As per the coastal regulation zone notifications, only repair of structures authorized prior to 1991 is permissible and no new construction is possible. Therefore, all the house owners of fully damaged and partly damaged katcha and pucca houses within 200 m of the High Tide Line, will be given the choice to go beyond 200 m, and get a newly constructed house worth Rs.1.50 lakh free of cost. Those who do not choose to do so will be permitted to undertake the repairs on their own in the existing locations.

Under the housing policy, about 1,30,000 families can be provided with concrete houses at an approximate cost of Rs.1,50,000/- each. Each houses will have 300-325 sq.ft of built up space. The houses will be having disaster resistant features. The lay out will have adequate infrastructure facilities like water supply, street lights, roads, rain water harvesting structures, drains, community centre, noon-meal centre, etc.

DISCRIMINATION IN PROVIDING RELIEF

The preliminary results of a survey conducted by the NGO People's watch—in Tamil Nadu in nine coastal villages in four tsunami-affected districts in early February—documented a pattern of caste-based discrimination in tsunami relief. The survey found that 7,796 individuals had been discriminatorily denied or excluded from government relief to which they were eligible. The most common reason reported for the denial was caste discrimination, followed by occupation, and religion. People's watch estimates that within each district the percentage of all those excluded from aid constitute from 1 to 8 per cent of the total number of tsunami-affected families.

There are widespread agreements among fishermen surveyed that the rich received better attention and treatment than the poor. Many complained that within their communities, wealthy fishermen who own expensive, sophisticated fishing boats receive more public and private assistance than bonded labourers who could not secure any benefits despite the fact that they had also lost all their assets. One poor fisherman commented, "The tsunami did not discriminate against people in its devastation but the rich and powerful have discriminated against us in securing aid". This remark may be even more apt with regard to dalits and those occupying the lower social status than with regular fishermen in coastal communities.

RELIEF PACKAGES PROVIDED BY GOVERNMENT

Immediately after the tsunami, the Tamil Nadu state government, local authorities and NGOs established temporary shelters for those displaced by the destruction. The central government established a one-time relief package for all the tsunami affected families that consisted of a cash grant of Rs.4,000 (US$91.95), along with rice, fuel, and basic household supplies (cooking stoves, vessels, for fetching water, etc.,) for the next three months (February, March and April), the government issued an individual relief package of Rs.1,000 (approximately US$23) and material relief worth Rs.526 (US$12) to tsunami–affected families. The government established a special relief fund from which the next of kin for each decreased family member received a one-time payment of Rs.100,000 each to next of kin for a family member tsunami casualty. In addition to death payments, the government announced it would compensate owners of machine boats between Rs.3,00,000 and Rs.5,00,000 depending on the extent of damage. Compensation for fibreglass boats and catamarans was less (Rs.25,000/-, 32,000/- or 75,000/- depending on the extent of damage).

More than 90 per cent of the deaths and property damage occurred in coastal fishing villages that were located within 100 to 200 meters of the sea. The tsunami destroyed more than 2,00,000 homes in the country (190,000 of these in Tamil Nadu) and 83,788 boats (52,638 of these in Tamil Nadu), wiping out these coastal fisher communities. Inland areas were severely affected by the salt water, thousands of acres of agricultural land were damaged, mostly in Tamil Nadu. Throughout the affected areas more than nine hundred camps housed the approximately 600,000 of them in Tamil Nadu. The damage is estimated at Rs.11,533.1 crore (US$ 265 billion); Losses in Tamil Nadu totalled an estimated Rs.4,528.66 crore (US$ 104 billion).

Security appears to be good within fisher communities. The study points out some violence, created during tsunami incidents & rehabilitation. They are as follows.,

- Several fishers in Kanyakumari district mentioned an incident in which members of fishermen's associations were roughed up after they sought to obtain benefits from both the government and NGOs.

- Residents of the villages of Melamanakudy in Kanya-kumari District caught a policeman who tried to take away the gold ornaments from the tsunami- damaged hut of a fisherman and turned him over to the higher police officials. The policeman was subsequently dismissed from service.

Due to the unprecedented destruction, tourism had been badly affected in the district of Kanyakumari. The inflow of tourists had gone down by 90% of the normal arrivals damage to two ferries and jetty owned by poompuhar, thiruvalluvar statue, Kamarajar mandapam and Kamarajar memorial, Boat jetty at Manakudi kayal and damges to chothavilai beach.

Chapter 3

26th DECEMBER 2004 — EYEWITNESSES

The Tsunami that struck the Tamil Nadu coast as on 26th December, 2004 at about 10 a.m. astounded the whole world. It is the greatest tragedy of the century for the nation. It was new to the loving memories of the coastal people of Kanyakumari district and this district is one of the worst hit areas. Tsunami has affected most of the coastal villages. Among the villages Melamanakudi and Kelamanakudi villages are considered as the hamlet of Thengamputhur revenue village, in Agatheeswaram taluk. Both the villages are situated in the west coast of Arabian Sea and on the western bank of the river Pazhayar. Melamanakudi and Kelamanakudi villages are village panchayats and administered by an elected panchayat President.

Post-tsunami the author wanted to know the housing and living conditions of families in Kelamanakudi and Melamanakudi villages of Kanyakumari district in 2010 within the framework.

Since post-tsunami housing conditions have to be disaster-resistant , a knowledge of vernacular housing and· building practices is essential. A comparative analysis of the costs and benefits of different building structures of various NGO's and their technologies was carried out. A reparability assessment of the housing structures in two tsunami-affected villages, and an appraisal of the quality of construction of post-tsunami housing projects was also done.

Kanyakumari District is one of the small districts of Tamil Nadu. This District is situated at the extreme south of the Indian subcontinent, the coastline is formed nearly by three seas, namely, Arabian Sea, Indian Ocean and Bay of Bengal. But the main part of the coast faces the Arabian Sea. The coastal landscape of Kanyakumari District is mainly composed of beach ridges of rocky, sandy and swampy nature in the estuarine regions. After independence, a people's movement demands to merge the district with Tamil Nadu, resulted in the constitution of the state Re-organization commission in 1956. Based on its recommendations, the Indian parliament passed the State Reorganization Act in March 1956 according to which the four taluks of Agastheeswaram, Thovalai, Kalkulam and Vilavancode were grouped to form a new "Kanyakumari District" on November 1, 1956. The district is divided into two revenue divisions Padmanabhapuram and Nagercoil having the headquarters at Thuckalay and Nagercoil respectively. There are 56 town Panchayats, 99 village Panchayats.

According to 2001 census in Kanyakumari District of Tamil Nadu, the population is 16,76,034 comprising of 832269 males and 663765 females.

On 26th December 2004 a massive earthquake measuring 8.5 on the Richter scale struck the coastal villages of Kanyakumari District due to the formation of High tidal waves (tsunami). Incalculable damage was caused to both lives and properties in the 33 coastal belt villages. The Tsunami has now added a new dimension to the people along the coast for their safety and welfare issues. Among these Melamanakudi and Kelamanakudi are the worst affected villages, the hamlet of Thengamputhoor Revenue village in Agastheewaram taluk.

The total population of Melamanakudi is 5793 as per the census available at Village Panchayat. Out of them 2929 are male and 2864 are female. There are nearly 1050 families in this village. As per Kelamanakudi village panchayat, in Kelamanakudi, the total population is 3,322 as per the recent census. There are 1451 male and 1871 female and 788 houses are there in this village. Apart from this TATA Colony has built 180 houses for this village. The main occupation is fishing, and due to tsunami most of the people living nearby the seashore lost their lives and belongings.

In order to obtain a correct information on the damage caused by the tsunami and to provide relief and rehabilitation measures to the people, the following work was carried out systematically in the two villages of Kelamanakudi and Melamanakudi.

- To assess the damages and losses incurred by the Tsunami affected coastal communities in the selected areas.

- To assess the extent of damage to the material needed for their livelihood.

- To assess the loss of dwelling units, material loss and damages of households.

- To ensure relief amounts fully benefiting children, women and families and evaluating the relief items received from the various organisations.

- To identify the specific needs of the people to be incorporated in the rehabilitation.

- To analyse the housing structure, the acceptability and their feeling at their new houses.

- To examine the damages found in the post tsunami housing structures.

- To find out the suggestions and improve the living conditions of the selected victim area.

Design is the process of making decision before a situation arises in which the decision has to be carried out. It is a process of deliberate anticipation directed towards bringing an unexpected situation under control—Russel Ackoft. Design is a plan of action.

In order to gain first hand information from the people of the respective villages, an interview schedule was prepared. The interview schedule contained questions relating to personal and family particulars, occupational particulars, things lost due to tsunami, materials received from Government and NGOs, Health condition before and after tsunami, present needs to enlighten their lives etc. The interview schedule was administered in the village of Melamanakudi and Kelamanakudi and it took about 25–30 minutes per respondent. The author went to the Melamanakudi & Kelamanakudi villages and received various informations regarding the living condition of the tsunami affected families and prepared an interview schedule.

The interview schedule was put on test on 50 respondents. On the basis of experience gained from testing the interview schedule, some modifications and questions were carried and the interview schedule was finalized.

INTERVIEW SCHEDULE

The interview schedule details on general information, household characteristics, damage to assets and entitlement, particulars of post-tsunami housing condition, housing preferences in post-tsunami, satisfaction of housing facilities, post tsunami living condition, present condition of their life and the needs to enlighten their future living condition etc.,

Two villages have been selected by the author to know the post-tsunami housing and living conditions. TATA, RUC, has constructed 369 houses in Kelamanakudi and 381 houses have been built in Melamanakudi by Navajeevan, YMCA and KSSS. In this, TATA colony has constructed 186, RUC 183, Navajeevan 52, YMCA 70 and KSSS 259 houses in these villages. A sample of 25% houses built by each NGO has been selected by the author. So, 47 houses from TATA colony (out of 186), 46 houses from RUC (out of 183) Navajeevan 13 (out of 52), YMCA 18 (out of 70) and in KSSS Colony 65(out of 259) totals 189 houses have been selected. The houses have been selected randomly and are from the affected villages in Kanyakumari District. . Interviews are conducted at the village level and the key informants are from the community. All categories of respondents such as elderly, disabled, women who have lost the breadwinners and Village Panchayat leaders are also interviewed.

FIELD VISIT

After the preparation of interview schedule the author visited the Melamanakudi & Kelamanakudi villages and made a personal interview with 189 house respondents.

DATA PROCESSING

The filled up interview schedules have been checked thoroughly and edited to make them complete for further processing. For proper arrangement of data a master table (coding sheet) containing all information has been prepared. Analysis and interpretation of data can be made with the help of the master table.

Even though the author was able to collect the required information from the respective villages, he was bound by the following limitations.

- The time taken for the work was limited.
- The sample size was also limited to only 189 members due to limited time.
- Source of the questions wereclosed and open-ended types and does not give room for elaborate answers.
- Parish priest was not appointed for 9 months in the Kelamanakudi village. Hence proper information could not be obtained during the work.

Chapter 4

ROLE OF NGOs—HOUSING AND RELIEF MEASURES

This chapter is an exclusive study of the role of various NGOs such as TATA, RUC, YMCA Navajeevan and KSSS colony in resettling the Tsunami victims by providing them with housing and relief measures. In Melamanakudi 47 TATA construction houses, 46 of RUC construction houses and in Kelamanakudi 18 houses from YMCA colony, 13 houses from Navajeevan, and 65 houses from KSSS colony were selected.A reparability assessment of the housing structures in two tsunami-affected villages, and an appraisal of the quality of construction of the post-tsunami housing projects was made.

STATISTICAL TOOLS

Statistical tools are playing an important role in the presentation of data in a simple manner and easy to understand to any one who look at it. In this chapter, tables have been used for the analysis of data.

In addition to the statistical information regarding the damage done to the houses and relief measures, a general information on the sex-wise distribution, details of the aged and disabled persons, types of houses and the ownership of houses is also provided in the tables (from Table 1.1 to Table 1.5). The figures in parentheses appearing in every table indicate percentage. The Table 1.1 shows sex-wise distribution of the sample respondents belonging to TATA, RUC, YMCA, Navajeevan and KSS Colony building structures.

It shows that 35.98% respondents are male, in which 21 (30.88%) of TATA housing, 19 (27.94%) of RUC in Kelamanakudi village and 6 (8.82%) of YMCA, 3 respondents (4.42%) of Navajeevan and 19 (27.94%) belong to Melamanakudi village. 64.02% are female, in which 26 (21.48%) of TATA housing, 27 (22.32%) of RUC and 12 of YMCA (9.92%) in Kelamanakudi village and 10 (8.26%) Navajeevan housing and 46 (38.02%) of KSSS housing belongs to Melamanakudi village. The Table reveals that the majority of the respondents are female.

The Table 1.2 represents the aged persons of Melamanakudi and Kelamanakudi villages.

There are 40 (21%) respondents between the age of 60 and 65. In this, 3 (6.38%) of them live in TATA housing, 6 (13.04%) of them live in RUC housing of Kelamanakudi village and 11 (61.1%) in YMCA, 6 (46.15%) respondents dwell in Navajeevan and 14 (21.5%) respondents live in KSSS housing of Melamanakudi village.

The aged persons between the age of 66 and 70 are 27 (14.28%). Only 12 (26.08%) respondents of RUC live in this age group at Kelamanakudi village and 2 (15.38%) of them in Navajeevan; 13 (6.87%) in KSSS colony. The persons at the age of above 71 cover 9 %, only four respondents (8.51%) live in TATA housing at Kelamanakudi village and three respondents (16.6%) dwell in YMCA and 2 (3.07%) respondents of KSSS live in Melamanakudi village.

Table 1.1 Sex-wise Distribution

Sex	Kelamanakudi			Melamanakudi		Total
	TATA	RUC	YMCA	NAVA JEEVAN	KSSS	
Male	21 (30.88)	19 (27.94)	6 (8.82)	3 (4.42)	19 (27.94)	68 (35.98)
Female	26 (24.48)	27 (22.32)	12 (9.92)	10 (8.26)	46 (38.02)	121 (64.02)
Total	47 (24.87)	46 (24.34)	18 (9.52)	13 (6.89)	65 (34.39)	189 (100)

Source: Primary Data

Table 1.2 Details of Aged Person

Aged Persons	Kelamanakudi			Melamanakudi		Total
	TATA	RUC	YMCA	NAVA JEEVAN	KSSS	
60–65	3 (6.38)	6 (13.04)	11 (61.1)	6 (46.15)	14 (21.5)	40 (21)
66–70	-	12 (26.08)	-	2 (15.38)	13 (6.87)	27 (14.28)
71 above	4 (8.51)	-	3 (16.6)	-	2 (3.07)	9 (4.76)
Total	47	46	18	13	65	189

Source: Primary Data

Table 1.3 Details of Disabled Person

No.of Disabled Person	Kelamanakudi			Melamanakudi		Total
	TATA	RUC	YMCA	NAVA JEEVAN	KSSS	
Handicapped	3 (6.38)	6 (13.04)	1 (5.55)	2 (15.38)	5 (7.7)	17
Total	47	46	18	13	65	189

Source: Primary Data

Table 1.4 Type of Houses

Type of Homes	Kelamanakudi			Melamanakudi		Total
	TATA	RUC	YMCA	NAVA JEEVAN	KSSS	
Thatched	3 (6.38)	-	-	-	-	3
Tiled	28 (59.5)	12 (26.08)	8 (44.4)	6 (46.15)	29 (44.6)	83
Concrete	16 (34.04)	34 (74)	10 (55.5)	7 (53.8)	36 (55.3)	103
Total	47	46	18	13	65	189

Source: Primary Data

The Table 1.3 details the disabled persons of Mela-manakudi and Kelamanakudi villages. There are 17 physically challenged respondents living in these villages. 3 (6.38%) in TATA housing, 6 (13.04%) in RUC, 1 (5.55%) at YMCA, 2 (15.38%) in Navajeevan and 5 (5.5%) in KSSS housing area.

The Table 1.4 provides the information on the type of houses the people lived before Tsunami. In Kelamanakudi village, 3 of them (6.38%) lived in thatched homes, 28 (59.5%) in tiled homes; 16 (34.04%) lived in concrete houses who have presently shifted to TATA housing. In RUC housing, 12 (26.08%) lived in tiled, and 34 (74.0%) have lived in concrete homes.

In Melamanakudi village, 8 (44.4%) lived in tiled covers, 10 (55.5%) in concrete houses covers are now living in YMCA houses. The Navajeevan and KSSS housing sector respondents have lived in tiled and concrete structures. 6 (46.15%) and 7 (53.8%) respondents lived in tiled, 29 (44.6%) and 36 (55.3%) lived in concrete buildings.

The ownership of house represents the Table 1.5.

The Table shows the ownership of house in both villages before tsunami. 47 (24.86%) of TATA housing, 46 (24.33%) of RUC, 18 (9.52%) of them at Navajeevan, and 65 (34.39%) of them are with KSSS.

Table 1.5 Ownership of House

Ownership of Home	Kelamanakudi		Melamanakudi			Total
	TATA	RUC	YMCA	NAVA JEEVAN	KSSS	
Own	47 (24.66)	46 (24.33)	18 (9.52)	13 (6.87)	65 (34.39)	189
Rented	-	-	-	-	-	-
Leased out	-	-	-	-	-	-
Total	47	46	18	13	65	189

Source: Primary Data

Table 1.6 Estimation of damage to the houses

Damages to Home	Kelamanakudi		Melamanakudi			Total
	TATA	RUC	YMCA	NAVA JEEVAN	KSSS	
Partially	-	7 (25.92)	2 (7.42)	-	18 (66.6)	27 (14.28)
Fully	47 (29.01)	39 (24.07)	16 (9.87)	13 (8.03)	47 (29.01)	162 (85.71)
Total	47	46	18	13	65	189

Source: Primary Data

The Table 1.6 estimates the damage to the houses during Tsunami in the selected villages of study. While analysing the village Kelamanakudi, occupants of the 47 (29.01%) houses that were completely destroyed during tsunami are now living in TATA housing, 7 (25.92%) houses were partially destroyed and 39 (24.07%) houses were fully destroyed in RUC housing sector. In Melamanakudi village, 2 (7.42%) houses were partially damaged and 16 (9.87%) of them were fully damaged in the YMCA section, 18 (66.66%) houses were partially damaged and 47 (29.02%) were fully damaged houses in KSSS. 13 (8.03%) houses were fully damaged in Navajeevan.

The Table 1.7 lists the damages of household assests/ possessions during Tsunami. Both the villages were severely affected by Tsunami. 100% of the electric fan was destroyed. 37 (78.72%) and 41 (89.13%) television set; 47(100%), 36 (76.26) wooden furniture; 32(68.08%), 21 (45.65%) steel furniture; 47(100%), 26 (56.52%) of stove; 19 (40.42%), 24 (52.17%) of academic certificate; 47(100%), 42 (91.30%) of books; 33 (70.21%) 39 (84.78%) kattumaram; 18 (38.29%), 19 (41.30%) vallam; and 39 (82.97%), 43 (93.47%) fishing nets were destroyed completely in TATA and RUC colony.

Table 1.7 Details of Lists the Damages of Household Assets/ Possessions

S.No	Items	Kelamanakudi TATA			RUC		
		Partially	Fully	No damage	Partially	Fully	No damage
01	Electric Fan		47 (100)			46 (100)	
02	Television		37 (78.72)			41 (89.13)	
03	Gas Stove		19 (40.42)		8 (17.39)	23 (50.00)	
04	Telephone		12 (25.53)			11 (23.91)	
05	Cell Phone		6 (12.76)			16 (34.78)	
06	Grinder		14 (29.78)			7 (15.21)	
07	Mixer Grinder		3 (6.38)			6 (13.04)	
08	Wooden Furniture		47 (100)		10 (21.73)	36 (76.26)	
09	Steel Furniture		32 (68.08)			21 (45.65)	
10	Washing Machine		3 (6.38)			7 (15.21)	
11	Stove		47 (100)		14 (30.43)	26 (56.52)	

12	Jewellery	3 (6.38)		8 (17.39)
13	Clothes	42 (89.36)		43 (93.47)
14	Educational Certificates	19 (40.42)	11 (23.91)	24 (52.17)
15	Ration Card	23 (48.93)		13 (28.26)
16	Bank Documents	3 (6.38)		7 (15.21)
17	Books	47 (100)		42 (91.30)
18	Two Wheeler	12 (25.76)		16 (34.78)
19	Cycle	6 (12.76)		19 (41.30)
20	Fibre Boat	-		-
21	Boat	-		-
22	Kattumaram	33 (70.21)		39 (84.78)
23	Vallam	18 (38.29)		19 (41.30)
24	Fish Nets	39 (82.97)		43 (93.47)
Total		47		46

S.No	Items	Melamanakudi								
		YMCA			NAVAJEEVAN			KSSS		
		Partially	Fully	No damage	Partially	Fully	No damage	Partially	Fully	No damage
01	Electric Fan		13 (100)			13 (100)		11(16.92)	47 (72.30)	
02	Television	7 (38.8)	6 (33.33)		2 (15.38)	9 (69.23)			51 (78.46)	
03	Gas Stove	3 (16.6)	11 (61.11)			10 (76.92)			49 (75.38)	
04	Telephone		7 (38.8)			6 (46.15)			18 (27.69)	
05	Cell Phone		2 (11.1)			4 (30.76)			29 (44.61)	
06	Grinder	6 (33.3)	9 (50)		3 (23.07)	7 (53.84)		11 (16.92)	47 (72.30)	
07	Mixer Grinder	3 (16.6)				2 (15.38)			19 (29.23)	
08	Wooden Furniture	3 (16.6)	10 (55.55)			11 (84.61)		11 (16.92)	49 (75.38)	
09	Steel Furniture	6 (33.3)	7 (38.8)			9 (69.23)		21(32.30)	34 (52.30)	

#	Item						
10	Washing Machine	4 (22.2)	2 (11.1)	4 (30.76)	3 (23.07)	8 (12.30)	12 (18.46)
11	Stove	4 (22.2)	13 (72.2)		11 (84.61)		58 (89.23)
12	Jewellery		2 (11.1)		-		12 (18.46)
13	Clothes		18 (100)		13 (100)		59 (90.76)
14	Educational Certificates	7 (38.8)	4 (22.2)		6 (46.15)	16 (24.61)	41 (63.07)
15	Ration Card	4 (22.2)	9 (50)		7 (53.84)		23 (35.38)
16	Bank Documents		6 (33.3)		5 (38.46)		6 (9.23)
17	Books	4 (22.2)	11 (61.11)		13 (100)	12 (18.46)	48 (73.84)
18	Two Wheeler		13 (72.2)		6 (46.15)	19 (29.23)	16 (24.61)
19	Cycle		11 (61.1)		9 (69.23)	16 (24.61)	31 (47.69)
20	Fibre Boat		-		-		-

S.No	Items	Melamanakudi								
		YMCA			NAVAJEEVAN			KSSS		
		Partially	Fully	No damage	Partially	Fully	No damage	Partially	Fully	No damage
21	Boat		-			-			-	
22	Kattu-maram		16 (88.8)			9 (69.23)			42 (64.61)	
23	Vallam		9 (50)			6 (46.15)			36 (55.38)	
24	Fish Nets		16 (88.8)			11 (84.61)			53 (81.53)	
Total		18			13			65		

In Melamanakudi, 100% of the electric fan was destroyed. 6 (33.33%),9 (69.23%), 51(78.46%) television set; 11(61.11%), 10(76.92%), 49 (75.38%) of gas stoves, 9 (50%) and 7 (53.84%), 47 (72.30%) grinders, 10(55.55%), 11 (84.61%), 49(75.38%) of wooden furniture; 7 (38.8%), 9(69.23%), 34(52.30%) of steel furniture; 13(72.2%), 11 (84.1%), 58(89.23%) of stove; 9(50%), 7(53.84%), 23(35.38%) of academic certificate; 11(61.10%), 13(100%), 48(73.83%) of books;11(61.11%), 9(69.23%), 31 (47.69%) of bicycles; 16(88.80%), 9 (69.23%),42 (64.61%) of kattumaram; 9(50 %), 6 (46.15%), 36(55.38%) of vallam; 16 (88.8%), 11(84.61%) and 53(81.53%) of fishing nets were fully destroyed in YMCA, Navajeevan and KSSS colony.

The partially damages items of RUC colony are 8 (17.39 %) gas stove, 10 (21.73%) wooden furniture, 14 (30.43%) stove and 11 (23.91%) of academic certificates. In YMCA, 7 (38.80%) television, 3 (16.6%) gas stove, 6(33.30%) grinders, 3(16.60%) mixer grinder, 6(33.30%) steel furniture, 4 (22.2 %) washing machine, 4 (22.2%) stove, 7 (38.8%) academic certificates, 4 (22.2%) ration card, 4 (22.2%) books were partially destroyed.

In Navajeevan Colony, 2 (15.38%) television, 3 (23.37 %) grinder, 4 (30.76%) washing machine were partially damaged. In KSSS Colony, 11 (16.92%) of electric fan, grinders and wooden furniture, 21(32.80%) steel furniture, 16 (24.61%) academic certificates, 19 (29.23%) two wheelers have been partially destroyed.

The Table 1.8 shows the details of stay of the respondents of Kelamanakudi and Melamanakudi after tsunami.

Table 1.8 Details of Respondents Stay After Tsunami

Reside After Tsunami	Kelamanakudi		Melamanakudi			Total
	TATA	RUC	YMCA	NAVAJEEVAN	KSSS	
Relative House	-	-	-	-	-	-
Friend House	-	-	-	-	-	-
Relief House	-	-	-	-	-	-
School Campus	-	-	18 (29.51)	13 (21.31)	30 (49.18)	61 (82.28)
College	-	-	-	-	-	-
Community Hall	47 (36.71)	46 (38.93)	-	-	35 (27.33)	128 (67.72)
Total	47	46	18	13	65	189

Source: Primary Data

Out of 189 respondents, 61 (32.28%) and 128 (67.72%) of them stayed at schools and in community halls. The respondents of Kelamanakudi 47 (36.71%) and 46 (38.93%) stayed in community hall at Thenthamaraikulam. In Melamanakudi, 18 (29.51%) respondents of YMCA, 13 (21.31 %) respondents of Navajeevan, 30 (49.18%) respondents of KSSS stayed at schools in Kottar and Ramanputhur. 35 (27.33 %) respondents of KSSS stayed at community hall.

The Table 1.9 measures the satisfaction on temporary accommodation. The TATA and RUC housing sector respondents of Kelamanakudi village and YMCA, Navajeevan and KSSS respondents of Melamanakudi village are fully satisfied with the temporary accommodation provided to them.

47 (24.86 %) respondents of TATA housing, 46 (24.33%) of RUC, 18 (9.53%), 13 (6.88%) and 65 (34.39%) of YMCA, Navajeevan and KSSS were satisfied with the temporary accommodation.

It reveals that 100% of the respondents are satisfied with the temporary accommodation provided to them.

The Table 1.10 shows the respondent satisfaction on the facilities at the temporary accommodation. The TATA and RUC housing sector respondents of Kelamanakudi village and YMCA, Navajeevan and KSSS respondents of Melamanakudi village are satisfied with the basic facilities provided at the temporary accommodation.

Table 1.9   Details of Respondent Satisfaction on Temporary Accommodation

Temporary Accommodation	KELAMANAKUDI		MELAMANAKUDI			Total
	TATA	RUC	YMCA	NAVAJEEVAN	KSSS	
Yes	47 (24.86)	46 (24.33)	18 (9.53)	13 (6.88)	65 (34.39)	189
No	-	-	-	-	-	-
Total	47	46	18	13	65	189

Source: Primary Data

Table 1.10   Details of Respondent Satisfaction on Facilities at the Temporary Accommodation

Facilities at the Temporary Accommodation	Kelamanakudi		Melamanakudi			Total
	TATA	RUC	YMCA	NAVAJEEVAN	KSSS	
Yes	47 (24.86)	46 (24.33)	18 (9.53)	13 (6.88)	65 (34.39)	189
No	-	-	-	-	-	-
Total	47	46	18	13	65	189

Source: Primary Data

Table 1.11 Details of Relief Items

Relief Items	Kelamanakudi		Melamanakudi			Total
	TATA	RUC	YMCA	NAVAJEEVAN	KSSS	
Monetary Benefit	47 (100)	46 (100)	18 (100)	13 (100)	65 (100)	189 (100)
Household Things	47 (100)	46 (100)	18 (100)	13 (100)	65 (100)	189 (100)
Education Benefit	29 (61.70)	41 (89.13)	12 (66.6)	9 (69.23)	49 (75.38)	140 (74.00)
Scholarship	15 (31.91)	29 (63.04)	8 (44.4)	18 (61.53)	36 (55.38)	121 (64.02)
House Construction	47 (100))	46 (100)	18 (100)	13 (100)	65 (100)	121 (64.02)
Vocational Training	20 (61.70)	37 (80.43)	11 (61.11)	6 (46.15)	31 (47.69)	121 (64.02)
Medical Relief	47 (100)	46 (100)	18 (100)	13 (100)	65 (100)	121 (64.02)
Total	47	46	18	13	65	189

Source: Primary Data

47 (24.86%) respondents of TATA housing, 46 (24.33%) of RUC, 18 (9.53%), 13 (6.88%) and 65 (34.39%) of YMCA, Navajeevan and KSSS colony were satisfied with the facilities. It reveals that 100% of the respondents are satisfied with facilities provided to them in the temporary accommodation.

The Table 1.11 explains the relief items provided to the selected village for research. Out of 189 respondents, the monetary benefit, household things, house construction and medical relief were given to both the villages. 47 (100%) of TATA, 46 (100%) of RUC, 18 (100%) of YMCA, 13 (100%) and 65(100%) of KSSS colony received the relief items. 29 (61.70 %) of TATA, 41 (89.13%) of RUC, 12 (66.6%) of YMCA, 9 (69.23%) of Navajeevan colony, 49 (75.38) of KSSS colony respondents received the education benefit. 15 (31.91%) of TATA, 29 (63.04%) of RUC, 8 (44.4%) of YMCA, 18 (61.53%) of Navajeevan and 36 (55.38%) of KSSS respondents received the scholarships.

The respondents have also received food, clothes, household things, hygienic kits, rice, groceries, utensils, fans, grinder stone, cupboard, sanitary napkin, sewing machine, play materials, school bags and toilet soaps as relief items.

The Table 1.12 shows the distribution of benefits to the people. 47 (100%) of TATA, 46 (100%) of RUC, 18 (100%) of YMCA, 13 (100%) and 65(100%) of KSSS colony received the relief items directly.

The Table 1.13 shows whether the people face any problem while receiving benefits. 47 (100%) of TATA, 46 (100 %) of RUC, 18 (100%) of YMCA, 13 (100%) and 65 (100%) of KSSS colony respondents did not find any problem in receiving the benefits.

Table 1.12 Distribution of Benefits

Distribution of Benefits	Kelamanakudi			Melamanakudi		Total
	TATA	RUC	YMCA	NAVAJEEVAN	KSSS	
Directly	47 (24.86)	46 (24.33)	18 (9.53)	13 (6.88)	65 (34.39)	189
Indirectly	-	-	-	-	-	-
Total	47	46	18	13	65	189

Source: Primary Data

Table 1.13 Problem in receiving Benefits

Problems in Receiving Benefits	Kelamanakudi			Melamanakudi		Total
	TATA	RUC	YMCA	NAVAJEEVAN	KSSS	
Yes	-	-	-	-	-	-
NO	47 (24.86)	46 (24.33)	18 (9.53)	13 (6.88)	65 (34.39)	189
Total	47	46	18	13	65	189

Source: Primary Data

Table 1.14   Details of Respondent Satisfaction with the Benefits

Satisfaction with the Benefits	Kelamanakudi		Melamanakudi			Total
	TATA	RUC	YMCA	NAVAJEEVAN	KSSS	
Yes	47 (24.86)	46 4.33)	18 (9.53)	13 (6.88)	65 (34.39)	189 (100)
No	-	-	-	-	-	-
Total	47	46	18	13	65	189

Source: Primary Data

Table 1.15   Rehabilitation Favourable for Women

Rehabilitation Favourable for Women	Kelamanakudi		Melamanakudi			Total
	TATA	RUC	YMCA	NAVAJEEVAN	KSSS	
Yes	47 (24.86)	46 (24.33)	18 (9.53)	13 (6.88)	65 (34.39)	189 (100)
No	-	-	-	-	-	-
Total	47	46	18	13	65	189

Source: Primary Data

The Table 1.14 shows the whether the people are satisfied with the benefits. 47 (100%) of TATA, 46 (100%) of RUC, 18 (100%) of YMCA, 13 (100%) and 65(100%) of KSSS colony respondents are satisfied with the benefits.

The Table 1.15 shows the whether the rehabilitation is favourable for women.

While considering the women respondents of the selected colony, 27 (100%) of TATA, 46 (100%) of RUC, 18(100%) of YMCA, 13 (100%) and 65(100%) of KSSS colony stated that they are satisfied and the rehabilitation is favourable for them.

Women respondents received rice, dhal, cooking oil, coconut oil, salt, dry chilly, tea dust, masala powder, soap, kerosene, talcum powder, tooth paste, sarees, nighty, bed sheet, inner wear, towel, household vessels, hygienic kits, and sanitary napkin.

It also indicates that the rehabilitation is favourable for the children. 47 (100%) of TATA, 46 (100%) of RUC, 18 (100%) of YMCA, 13 (100%) and 65(100%) of KSSS colony respondents stated that the rehabilitation to the children are satisfactory.

The children received school bags, school kits, play materials and hygienic kits as rehabilitation.

In the initial stages after a disaster, trauma-related psychological and behaviour responses like acute stress reaction, disaster syndrome, grief reactions, withdrawal and even aggression, violence and conflict can occur. Some women respondents said that sometimes they hear the sound of the tsunami wave. They also said that they took shifts staying awake at night to keep watch and reassure their children. Psycho-social counselling, mental health counselling, children and adolescents counselling, and disease surveillance counselling sessions were conducted for the children during the Post-tsunami Period.

The Table 1.16 describes the factors contributing to change of living place.

26 (13.76%) are willing to move to the newly constructed houses due to fear of tsunami. 95 (50.26%) of the respondent are aware of disaster management and 68 (35.98%) for want of better lifestyle.

Housing is the subsequent prime need for the people who are affected in the Tsunami. The particulars of post-tsunami housing conditions differ from place to place. The TATA, RUC, and Navajeevan housing colonies are 3 km far from their old residence. Subsequently, YMCA and KSSS colonies are 2 km away from their residence. The houses were allocated only after 2½ years to the TATA, RUC, YMCA, Navajeevan and KSSS Colony respondents.

In the process of housing preference in post-tsunami, out of 189 respondents in the selected sample 100% of the people gave petition to the District Administrative, Kanyakumari District for want of a new house.

The community leader who has direct experience with the Tsunami devastation at the relief and reconstruction stage represents the views of the community and has the ability to influence the decision process on activities for the community.

Lottery method is used for allocation of houses which was constructed by NGOs. A meeting was conducted in the presence of District Collector, Bishop and the members of various NGOs. The respondents then received their allotted house key and occupied their respective homes on an auspicious day.

Table 1.16 Factors Contributing to Change of Living Place

Factors	Kelamanakudi			Melamanakudi		Total
	TATA	RUC	YMCA	NAVAJEEVAN	KSSS	
Fear of Tsunami	3 (11.54)	6 (23.08)	-	2 (7.69)	15 (57.69)	26 (13.76)
Awareness of disaster management	32 (33.68)	29 (30.54)	8 (8.42)	5 (5.26)	21 (22.10)	95 (50.26)
Better life style	12 (17.65)	11 (16.18)	10 (14.71)	6 (8.82)	29 (42.64)	68 (35.98)
Total	47	46	18	13	65	189

Table 1.17 Respondent Satisfaction on Housing Structure

Satisfaction on Housing Structure	Kelamanakudi			Melamanakudi		Total
	TATA	RUC	YMCA	NAVAJEEVAN	KSSS	
Yes	11 (18.96)	3 (5.17)	0	2 (3.45)	42 (72.42)	58 (30.69)
No	36 (27.49)	43 (32.82)	18 (13.74)	11 (8.39)	23 (17.56)	131 (69.31)
Total	47	46	18	13	65	189

Source: Primary Data

The Table 1.17 elucidates whether the respondents are satisfied with the housing structure. Out of 189 respondents, 58 (30.69%) are satisfied with their housing structure on the other hand 131 (69.31%) respondents are not satisfied with the arrangements provided in the housing structure. In this 11 (18.96%) of TATA; 3 (5.17%) of RUC of Kelamanakudi village, 2 (3.45%) of Navajeevan; and 42 (72.42%) of KSSS colony belongs to Melamanakudi village appreciated the housing structure.

36 (27.49%) of TATA colony; 43 (32.82%) of RUC belongs to Kelamanakudi village, 18 (13.74%) of YMCA; 11(8.39) of Navajeevan; 23 (17.56%) of KSSS Colony belongs to Melamanakudi village are not satisfied with the housing structural methods.

It has been observed that there are no separate rooms available for couples and children. There is no provision for study and living purposes. The kitchen is not constructed with proper ventilation and without adequate work area for cooking purposes.

The respondents believe in Vasthu Shasthram, they feel that the toilet/bathroom and staircase are not constructed according to it. It is in the north-east direction where water bodies must be placed.

Vastu Shastra ("science of construction") is a traditional Hindu system of design based on directional alignments. Vaastu Shastra combines all the five elements (Earth, Air, Water, Space and Fire) of nature and balances them with the person and the material.

It takes advantage of the benefits bestowed by the five elements of nature to create a congenial living and working environment thereby facilitating spiritual well-being and paving the way for enhanced health, wealth, prosperity and happiness.

There are damages and problems found in the post-tsunami housing colonies in the selected village. The house design should possess with a living room, dining room and bedroom with a kitchen, a small entrance verandah, a bathroom and a toilet. The RCC houses built by the NGOs have failed the idea and to appreciate the climatic and socio-cultural importance of this place.

The houses are designed to be modern but the houses are built in straight rows with less than four feet space between two rows gave little privacy to the respondents. Space around the house varies from site to site. The lack of space between structures would eventually become a fire hazard.

Respondents are also ignorant about details of house designs, materials and technology. People mentioned that no consultation took place with them. The building materials are not inspected for they are suitable to withstand climatic stress of the coast.

The kitchen is too small for them to work. There is not proper ventilation in the kitchen. The cement or tiled flooring is uneven. Proper polishing is not done. The walls are cracked in most of the houses. The staircase to terrace has cracked. There is not outlet pipe in the terrace that has resulted to dampness and leakage in the roof. The toilets are not built as per specifications and the septic tank is small and needs to be cleaned often. The drainage system has not been made wherever required. There is no outlet pipes provision in the houses for cleaning purposes.

The shelves are open and there is no provision of doors. The switch boards are not fixed properly and the poor quality switches are used. In some houses, electricity and water have been provided but are inadequate. The Electricity Reading Meter which is fixed is not of good quality.

There is no proper water supply and electricity facility at these houses. Water tap connections are not provided in most of the houses and they depend on Municipal water. There are very few municipal water taps and water is supplied for only a short duration. They need to store the water in tanks manually. Hence, water for individual households is not sufficient. The municipal authorities are providing water yet it is not sufficient to meet the needs of the entire community. Rainwater harvesting facility should be incorporated in community planning, so they also can depend upon rainwater harvesting in water tanks. People consistently complained that the RCC roof is damp and leaks during rain. Good quality wood is not used for door and windows. The materials used in the houses are not durable, waterproof and heat resistant.

Defective material used in these types of houses. There is no proper padlock available in the doors. The latch in the windows and door are not fixed properly. The grill in the window has space and uncovered or with a wire mesh, did not provide protection against flies, mosquitoes and other small insects. There is no provision of compound wall. The houses have been placed too close to each other, leaving no space to rear their livestock. Sanitation facilities including soak pits, septic plants, garbage collection points, composting areas and fish drying areas are not available at these sites.

The people are staying in the new houses about 2kms from their original habitat. Some respondents wish not to shift out of them since they are comfortable and do not want to move into newer areas of neighbourhood. At all areas, women and men complained about the inadequate size of the house. Couple, women and adolescent girls are the most affected, as there is no space for privacy. The Table 1.18 lists the problems that are faced in the post-tsunami housing colonies.

Table 1.18 Problems found in the Post Tsunami Housing Colonies

S.No	Problems	Kelamanakudi		Melamanakudi			Total
		TATA	RUC	YMCA	NAVAJEEVAN	KSSS	
1.	Flooring in Terrace is in very poor condition	38 (31.7)	36 (30)	12 (10)	8 (6.7)	26 (21.7)	120 (63.49)
2.	Toilet is less spacious and no bathroom facility	43 (26.70)	42 (26.09)	14 (8.69)	9 (5.59)	53 (32.92)	161 (85.19)
3	Less Depth of Sewage water tank	39 (26.17)	44 (29.5)	15 (10.06)	11 (10.06)	40 (26.8)	149 (78.84)
4	Lack of compound wall and insecurity	37 (30.08)	46 (37.39)	18 (14.63)	13 (10.56)	9 (7.32)	123 (65.08)
5	Cracks in the walls	18 (20.45)	31 (35.28)	15 (17.05)	11 (12.5)	13 (14.77)	88 (46.56)
6	Terrace poor out loft facility	41 (28.08)	46 (31.51)	18 (12.33)	13 (8.9)	28 (19.18)	146 (77.25)

S.No	Problems	Kelamanakudi			Melamanakudi			Total
		TATA	RUC	YMCA	NAVAJEEVAN	KSSS		
7	Improper Flooring	41 (29.71)	43 (31.16)	18 (13.04)	13 (9.42)	23 (16.67)		138 (73.02)
8	Non Provision of Loft	43 (35.83)	44 (36.67)	11 (9.17)	9 (7.5)	13 (10.83)		120 (63.49)
9	Cracks in Windows and Doors & Poor Quality Wood	39 (31.97)	32 (26.23)	15 (12.29)	13 (10.66)	23 (18.85)		122 (64.55)
10	No water proof doors	37 (30.58)	29 (23.96)	17 (14.05)	13 (10.74)	25 (20.67)		121 (64.02)
11	Non-vasthu based house constructed (toilet and bathrooms upstairs' steps)	43 (28.67)	29 (23.96)	17 (14.05)	13 (10.74)	25 (20.67)		121 (64.02)
12	Lack of Overhead Tank water supply	30 (26.55)	35 (30.97)	16 (14.16)	9 (17.96)	23 (20.36)		113 (59.79)
13	Insufficient space in the Kitchen	38 (31.67)	36 (30.00)	12 (10.00)	8 (6.67)	26 (21.67)		120 (63.49)

S.No	Problems	Kelamanakudi		Melamanakudi			Total
		TATA	RUC	YMCA	NAVAJEEVAN	KSSS	
14	Lack of space in bath room and washing area	43 (26.70)	42 (26.09)	14 (8.69)	9 (5.59)	53 (32.93)	161 (85.19)
15	Poor construction & building structure. NO Provision for future extension			18 (9.52)			
16	Weak Housing Basement	10 (12.5)	31 (38.75)	15 (18.75)	11 (13.75)	13 (16.25)	80 (42.33)
17	Improper Electrification	23 (21.11)	41 (37.61)	11 (10.09)	13 (11.93)	21 (19.27)	109 (57.67)
18	Poor quality padlocks in doors	30 (30.93)	31 (31.96)	16 (16.49)	9 (9.28)	11 (11.34)	97 (51.32)
19	Improper drainage facility inside the house	39 (31.71)	35 (28.46)	13 (10.57)	13 (10.57)	23 (18.69)	123 (65.08)

S.No	Problems	Kelamanakudi			Melamanakudi			Total
		TATA	RUC	YMCA	NAVAJEEVAN	KSSS		
20	Leakage of roofs during rainy seasons	8 (9.88)	35 (43.21)	16 (19.75)	9 (11.11)	13 (16.05)		81 (42.86)
21	Excess of heat due to unfinished terrace.				13			13 (6.88)
22	Improper Plastering and Painting	33 (26.19)	27 (21.43)	19 (15.08)	11 (8.73)	36 (28.57)		126 (66.67)
23	More homes extra kitchen arrangement by thatched huts to inside house (above fan). Hence	37 (27.4)	41 (30.3)	15 (11.1)	11 (8.2)	31 (22.9)		135 (71.43)
24	Poor construction of Hall	39 (33.3)	31 (26.4)	13 (11.1)	13 (11.1)	21 (18)		117 (61.9)
25	Lack of Loft and almirah for keeping things	37 (31.0)	35 (29.4)	11 (9.2)	9 (7.5)	27 (23)		119 (62.96)
Total		47	46	18	13	65		189

Most of the families have partitioned the room to separate it from the living space. They have additionally extended a kitchen, where some houses have enhanced bathrooms, and toilets. Some have extended their houses for the old and physically challenged persons who are unable to bear the heat under these structures.

The Table 1.19 pictures that 57 respondents have constructed single room; 10 respondents have constructed two rooms, 88 respondents have renovated their toilets and bathroom and 74 respondents have modified and extended their kitchen according to their needs.

Some Respondents have built compound wall that costs Rs. 50,000/-. They have changed the cement flooring to marble or tiled flooring. They have also changed the front wooden door. Wiring, electric connection, switch boards and padlock have been changed.

Most of them have changed the existing kitchen to dining or as a separate bed room and a new kitchen has been constructed according to their plan. In some houses they have constructed bathroom inside the house for safety purposes. They have paved tiles in the terrace to resist their house from heat and dampness. It is understood that the respondents have spent Rs. 65,000/- to Rs. 2,75,000/- for reconstructing their houses. They have borrowed money from money lenders with huge interest for renovating their houses.

It is imperative to notice in most of the cases the fishing communities do not have *pattas* or land rights and title deeds.

Table 1.19   Renovation construction in Post-tsunami Housing

Renovation Construction on Housing Structure	Kelamanakudi			Melamanakudi		Total
	TATA	RUC	YMCA	NAVAJEEVAN	KSSS	
Single Room	15 (26.00)	12 (21.00)	9 (16.00)	-	21 (37.00)	57 (100)
Two Room	6 (60.00)	-	-	-	4 (40.00)	10 (100)
Toilet & Bathroom	15 (17.00)	29 (33.00)	12 (14.00)	-	32 (36.00)	88 (100)
Kitchen	20 (27.00)	12 (16.00)	8 (11.00)	-	34 (46.00)	74 (100)

Source: Primary Data

Respondents have received the title deed which reflects a Joined Deed with the concerned Housing NGO.

Coastal communities depend on fishing for their livelihoods and it is necessary for them to live close to the coast. Respondents expressed their woes stating that they have to reside in a place from where they could see the sea because decisions on when to fish could be determined entirely by tidal and weather conditions. The Post Tsunami colonies are far away from the sea and it is very difficult for them to carry out fishing activities when they are far from the coast.

Fishing communities felt that they could not afford the increased transportation cost from the new relocation colony.

Similarly, if they live miles away from the coast, they are not comfortable leaving their boats and nets unattended on the shore without being able to watch over them. It has been also identified that the Fishing communities, who constitute over 80% of the affected people, resisted relocation and it also turned out to be virtually impossible to find sufficient land to rebuild all coastal villages in new locations.

It is disappointing to hear that the people complained that most agencies have built houses or endow with primary support after which there have been no contact with the community for feedback or they have been actually benefited from the support provided to them. They did not even know how to contact NGO members who are responsible for constructing their houses with their grievances.

The Table 1.20 indicates that the respondents have road and street light facility in their new housing area.

47 (100%) of TATA, 46 (100%) of RUC, 18 (100%) of YMCA, 13 (100%) and 65(100%) of KSSS colony respondents stated that they have proper road and street light facility available in their respective area.

The Table 1.21 explains that 100% of the respondents have also received their own ration card.

47 (100%) of TATA, 46 (100%) of RUC, 18 (100%) of YMCA, 13 (100%) and 65(100%) of KSSS colony respondents stated that they have received the new ration card.

Most of resettlement sites visited, in Kanyakumari District, seemed to have been planned with the idea of an urban slum in mind. It is essential that technical and quality guidelines for structure, construction materials used, and disaster resistant features are adequately dispersed. However, housing provided as part of a resettlement package is found to be grossly lacking in standards of habitability.

Table 1.20 Details of Proper Road and Street Light Facility

Proper Road and Street Light Facility	Kelamanakudi		Melamanakudi			Total
	TATA	RUC	YMCA	NAVAJEEVAN	KSSS	
Yes	47 (24.86)	46 (24.33)	18 (9.53)	13 (6.88)	65 (34.39)	189 (100)
No	-	-	-	-	-	-
Total	47	46	18	13	65	189

Source: Primary Data

Table 1.21 Issue of New Ration Card

New Ration Card	Kelamanakudi		Melamanakudi			Total
	TATA	RUC	YMCA	NAVAJEEVAN	KSSS	
Yes	47 (24.86)	46 (24.33)	18 (9.53)	13 (6.88)	65 (34.39)	189 (100)
No	-	-	-	-	-	-
Total	47	46	18	13	65	189

Source: Primary Data

Chapter 5

POST–TSUNAMI SCENARIO
AND SUGGESTIONS

The housing and living conditions of post-tsunami families in Kelamanakudi and Melamanakudi villages has been analysed by the author in this chapter. Various factors like post-tsunami housing structures built by NGO's, respondent views on Tsunami housing, evaluation if right standards housing structures are used in housing and enforced in developing adequate housing for the survivors has been carried out.

While the respondents were questioned on the problems faced in the post-tsunami housing colony, they stated that they faced lot of problems in the new settlement. As they believed in Vaasthu Shastra, they felt that the toilet/bathroom and staircase were not constructed according to it. It is in the north-east direction where water sump must be placed.

Vaastu Shastra ("science of construction") is a traditional Hindu system of design based on directional alignments. Vaasthu Shastra combines all the five elements (earth, air, water, space and fire) of nature and balances them with the person and the material.

It takes advantage of the benefits bestowed by the five elements of nature to create a congenial living and working environment thereby facilitating spiritual well-being and paving the way for enhanced health, wealth, prosperity and happiness.

The houses are designed to be modern but the houses are built in straight rows with less than four feet space between two rows giving little privacy to the respondents. Space around the house varies from site to site. The lack of space between structures would eventually become a fire hazard. Construction of compound wall is highly essential for their safety and security.

The kitchen is too small for them to work. There is not proper ventilation in the kitchen. The cement or tiled flooring is uneven. The walls are cracked in most of the houses. The staircase to terrace has also cracked. There is no outlet pipe in the terrace for the rain water to harvest. It results in dampness and leakages.

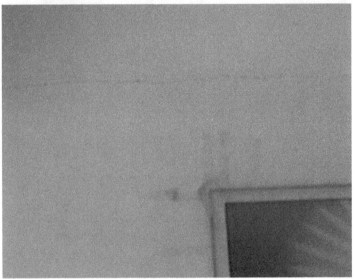

The toilets are not built as per specifications and the septic tank is too small that needs to be cleared often. The drainage system has not been made where required. There is no outlet pipes provision in the houses for cleaning purposes.

The shelves are open and there is no provision of doors. The switch boards are not fixed properly and poor quality switches are used. The Electricity Reading Meter which is fixed is not of good quality. The respondents have to change the meter frequently.

There is no proper water supply and electricity facility at these houses. Water tap connections are not provided in houses and they depend on panchayat water. There is very few panchyat water tap connection and water is supplied for only a short duration. They need to store the water in tanks manually. Hence, water for individual households is not sufficient. Rainwater harvesting facility should be incorporated in community planning, so they can depend on rainwater harvesting in water tanks. Sanitation does not exist in most of the houses. Defective materials have been used in these types of houses. There is no padlock available in the door. The latch in the windows and door are not fixed properly. The grill in the window has gap and not covered with a wire mesh, did not provide protection against flies, mosquitoes and other small insects.

The people are staying in the new houses about 2 km from their original habitat. Some respondents prefer not to shift out of them since they are comfortable and do not want to move into newer areas of neighbourhood. At all areas, women and men complained about the inadequate size of the house. Couple, women and adolescent girls are the most affected, as there is no space for privacy.

Most of the families have partitioned the room to separate it from the living space. They have additionally extended a kitchen, where some houses have built bathrooms and toilets. Some have extended their houses for the children, old and physically challenged persons who are unable to bear the heat under these structures.

Some respondents have built compound wall that costs Rs. 50,000/-. They have changed the cement flooring to marble or tiled flooring. They have also changed the front wooden door. Wiring, electric connection, switch boards and padlock have been changed.

Most of them have changed the existing kitchen to dining or as separate room and a new kitchen has been constructed according to their plan. They have put tiles on the terrace to resist their house from heat and dampness. The respondents have spent Rs. 60,000/- to Rs. 2,75,000/- for reconstructing their houses. Fishing communities do not have *pattas* or land rights and title deeds in most of the cases.

Fishing communities felt that they could not afford the increased transportation cost from the new relocation colony.

Similarly, if they live miles away from the coast, they are not comfortable leaving their boats and nets unattended on the shore without being able to watch over them. It has been also identified that the fishing communities, who constitute over 80% of the affected people, resisted relocation and it also turned out to be virtually impossible to find sufficient land to rebuild all coastal villages in new locations.

It is disappointing to hear that the people complained that most agencies who have built houses or endowed with primary support were not available for contact with the community for feedback or to know if they have been actually benefited from the support provided to them. They did not even know how to contact NGO members who are responsible for constructing their houses to raise their grievances.

100 percent of respondents indicated that they have road and street light facility in their new housing area and they have also received their own ration card.

SUGGESTIONS

In the Post-tsunami Housing programme, quality management has been one of the areas which did not receive adequate attention and has resulted in varying standards of houses, though there are systems, resources, as well as capacities to monitor the quality of houses constructed in large housing programmes.

A housing loan may be provided by the state government or by the Cooperative Society to individual house owners for them to renovate their houses according their economic condition and plan.

The housing project should ensure that the chosen site meets the requirements of Coastal Regulation Zone rules. All the housing projects should comply with the existing and future development plans of the area.

The design of individual houses should include maximum provision for natural light and adequate ventilation should be provided in the individual houses, particularly the kitchen, so as to avoid indoor air pollution.

Most of the houses lost in the tsunami belonged to the fishing community; the site of resettlement housing must be conducive to their needs. According to them, the house design should possess a living room, dining room and a kitchen, a small entrance verandah, a bathroom and a toilet. There must be an exclusive bed room for the married people. The RCC houses built by the NGOs have failed to appreciate the respondent ideas and the climatic and socio-cultural importance of this place.

The people must be aware of house designs, materials and technology. Proper consultation with them would enhance the housing structure and the quality of the house. The building materials must be inspected for their sustainability and suitability to withstand climatic stress of the coast.

People consistently complained that the RCC roof is damp and it leaks during rain. Good quality wood must be used for door and windows. The materials used in the houses must be durable, waterproof and heat resistant.

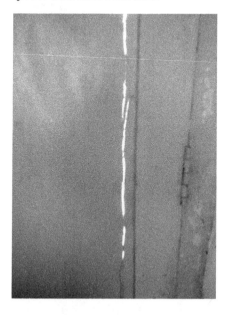

There must be provision for compound wall. There should be adequate space from one house to another to rear their livestock and for fish drying. Sanitation facilities including soak pits, septic plants, garbage collection points and composting areas are not available at these sites.

Though the panchayat authorities are providing water; it is not enough to meet the needs of the entire community. As an alternate, rainwater harvesting facility should be incorporated in community planning, so they can depend on rainwater harvesting in water tanks.

Overhead tank must be placed and adequate plumbing work should be executed. There must be outlet pipes fixed inside the house and in the terrace for cleaning purposes. The septic tank should be big in size for the joint family system.

Resettlement housing must be in a suitable location that must enable access to employment, primary health-care, food, education and other social services and civic amenities. In addition, the location must be safe, particularly from environmental hazards and pollutants.

A socio-economic survey and risk assessment study have to be conducted and model houses should be set up with the aim of creating a new habitat, and ensuring the protection of the fisherfolk.

After the Tsunami, people became psychologically weak and Tsunami shattered their hopes and aspirations in lives. In order to build confidence and hope for the future to people who were living at the stage of helplessness and hopelessness, a well thought out counselling program needs to be designed with the active participation of experts.

Coastal communities depend on fishing for their livelihoods and it is imperative that they continue to live close to the coast.

Respondents expressed their woes stating that they have to live in a place from where they could see the sea because decisions on catching fish can be determined entirely by tidal and weather conditions. The Post-tsunami colonies are far away from the sea and it is very difficult for them to carry out fishing activities when they are far from the coast.

Relief and rehabilitation requires assessment as well as monitoring and should involve local governing bodies. Joint task forces comprising of affected people, experts from various departments such as sociologists, psychologists, social workers and engineers., and members of the implementing agency should be set up for the purpose of rehabilitation.

A Community Development Organizer may be exclusively appointed in every tsunami affected villages by the State Government to observe the living condition, housing condition, rehabilitation and training programmes for the future development.

The victims aim for the alternate employment opportunities in the project area. They need alternate employment opportunities which to create self-employment for the tsunami affected youth and women.

Special programmes to address the needs of the vulnerable people – children, aged population, physically or mentally challenged, etc, which have the potential to improve quality of life of the fishers and many new rehabilitation programmes must be coming up over the next year to address women's needs more meaningfully.

CONCLUSION

From the beginning, the Government of Tamil Nadu and the District Authorities have played a crucial role in coordinating the relief and recovery work in an impressive manner. A number of NGOs and Resource Centres also helped them in their mission.

The continuing challenge is to restore and improve the previous living conditions of the affected communities. The key areas have been identified: individual and community rehabilitation, analyzing the housing construction, impact and needs of the community, recovery of women and children. As the Tsunami has destroyed lives, livelihood and properties, it turned out to be an opportunity to learn from the past.

The relief agencies should recognize that durable and culturally appropriate solutions can only be achieved through greater participation of the affected communities. All agencies durable also recognise that so far rehabilitation efforts have been more to their convenience and competence than what is actually needed. Needs and rights-based efforts would require far greater changes than their own thinking and practice.

The rehabilitation aims at replacing the lost assets. It would definitely brought a change in the mode of operations for the fishers, it would be necessary to discuss how adequate the support had been as otherwise it would be difficult for the fishers to adjust to the new set of conditions that the new operations imposed upon them.

In every way of post-tsunami scenario, non-governmental organisations have played a vital role in the relief and rehabilitation efforts and in construction of houses. There were many promising examples of the selfless services of the NGO workforce executed in many parts of the coast and these were much appreciated by the fishers. In fact, the fishers informed, the prompt arrival of the NGOs soon after the tsunami to undertake relief else their condition would have been worse.

On the other hand, it is also one of the tragedies of the rehabilitation phase studies were largely ignored while planning and implementing the programmes. It has been also identified that several NGOs dealt only with the panchayats and rarely interacted with the community people. The Panchayats should act as an interface between the communities and the rehabilitation agencies without affecting the scope and direction of the support programmes.

Agencies must follow internationally accepted human rights standards and principles in their work. A rights-based approach must underlie all relief and rehabilitation work and the principles of non-discrimination, equality, and gender sensitivity must be encouraged. Rehabilitation should explore the long-term needs and rights of individuals and communities. Rehabilitation policies must be culture sensitive and suitable in order to meet the local conditions.

The decisions regarding the size and design of the house and layout of the colony should be taken after consultation with the community. NGOs should ensure that there is a meaningful participation of the marginalized sections of the community including women, those belonging to ethnic and religious minorities, dalits, the elderly and the disabled.

Post Tsunami Houses must be constructed using socially and culturally appropriate processes and infrastructure designs, and should be disaster-sensitive and eco-friendly. Local materials favoured by the people should be used as far as possible. The new housing should be accessible to people with disabilities and to senior citizens.

Construction and design of the permanent house should allow for extensions. The total number of family members in a house must be considered when building and allocating new houses. Extended families that lived in one large house cannot be given the same space meant for a single family.

However, the massive house construction programme requires much scope existed for people to work. Earnest efforts may make the communities to involve for housing construction. The response would be lukewarm; few fishers would get involved, but a large majority tend to stay out of it.

NGOs should encourage and provide training in house construction to the communities. There would be due contribution in building their own houses.

Efforts could be made to ensure that members of fishing communities are able to live close enough to the sea could be able to continue their livelihood and also to have access to their boats and nets.

It is also essential, and an initiative step from the Government of Tamil Nadu that Woman must be granted joint ownership deeds in the name of the man and the woman of a household to the land on which the new houses were coming up.

The Tsunami not only destroyed lives and properties, but also had a devastating impact on the psyche of people. Any traumatic events can lead to acute and long-term mental health and psychosocial consequences. For the first time in living memory, the fishing community has developed a "fear of the sea".

However, the government has launched programmes focusing on issues like psychosocial care and child protection, the trauma that children and the women have undergone are quite extensive. Consequently, the Government can also initiate a periodic school-based counselling and community-based activities to help children recover from psychological distress.

A holistic habitat planning approach is the crux of Government of Tamil Nadu in facilitating the affected community. It is paramount in any reconstruction and recovery programme. It is essential that recovery and rehabilitation work, technical and quality guidelines, construction materials used, and disaster resistant features for structure must be focused on the long-term needs of the affected population in a holistic way.

BIBLIOGRAPHY

- **After the tsunami, Human Rights of vulnerable populations**, Human Right Center, University of California, Berkoley, East-West Center, October 2005.

- Arun Kumar Talwar; Satish Juneja: **Encyclopaedia of Disaster Management Cyclone Disaster Management**, New Delhi: Commonwealth Publishers, 2008 Vol.6.

- Arun Kumar Talwar; Satish Juneja: **Encyclopaedia of Disaster Management Tsunami Disaster Management**, New Delhi: Commonwealth Publishers, 2008.

- Arun Kumar Talwar; Satish Juneja: **Encyclopaedia of Disaster Management Flood Disaster Management,** New Delhi: Commonwealth Publishers, 2008 Vol.9.

- Arun Kumar Talwar; Satish Juneja: **Encyclopaedia of Disaster Management Global Climate Change,** New Delhi: Commonwealth Publishers, 2008 Vol.10.

- **Beyond the Turbulent Tide: Tsunami Emergency Assistance Project Livelihood Support Programme.** Chennai: Tamil Nadu Slum Clearance Board.

- Dr. Amit Awasthy. **Disaster Management Warning Response and Community Relocation,** New Delhi: Global India Publications Pvt. Ltd., 2009.

- Dr.S.L.Goel., **Disaster Administration Theory and Practice**, New Delhi: Deep & Deep Publications Pvt. Ltd., 2009.

- **From Disaster to Development: Activities Carried Out by The Government**, NGOs and INGOs for the Tsunami affected people in Kanyakumari District, Nagercoil: Kanyakumari Rehabilitation Resource Center.

- Gomathy, N.B., **The role of traditional Panchayats in coastal fishing communities in Tamil Nadu, with special reference to their role in mediating Tsumani relief and rehabilitation**, Proceedings from the ICSF Post-Tsunami Rehabilitation Workshop, January,2006.

- Iwan. W.D., **Summary report of the Great Sumatra Earthquakes and Indian Ocean tsunamis of 26 December 2004,** Earthquake Engineering Research Institute, EERI Publication 2006,

- Krishna, T. (2005). **"Tamil Nadu"**, Surya Books Private Limited, Chennai

- Mukesh Kapoor., **Disaster Management.**,New Delhi: Saurabh Publishing House, 2010.

- Nayak, Nalini and A.J. Vijayan., **The Coasts, the fish resources and the fishworkers' movement**, National Human Rights Commission. Government of India. 2006.

- **Project Implementation Plan Emergency Tsunami Reconstruction Project**, Tamil Nadu 2005.

- **Report from CRD of India**, Tsunami Rehabilitation Project, Kanyakumari District, Tamil Nadu, South India.

- Sawalia Bihari Verma, Sant Gyaneswar Prasad Singh, Shib Kumari Singh., **Rural Infrastructure Sanita-**

tion, Housing, Health Care. New Delhi: Sarup & Sons, 2008.

- Sawalia Bihari Verma; Sant Gyaneswar Prasad Singh; Shib Kumari Singh, **Rural Infrastructure: Sanitation Housing Health Care.**

- Sridhar, V. (2005). **"Living on the Edge"**, Frontline (Magazine published by Kastury and Sons Limited, Chennai), Vol. 22, No. 3, pp. 15-16.

- Staff Writer (27.01.2005) **Tsunami Aid: Who's Giving What,** Retrieved on 22.04.2006.

- Staff Writer, **"Clinton, Bush: Tsunami Aid Helping"**, The Early Show / CBS News, February 21, 2005

- **Tsunami Response "from Agony to Ecstasy",** Kottar Social Service Society (KSSS) – Report.

- **Tsunami: Wave of Change What We Can Learn from the Indian Ocean Tsunami of December 2004.** Scientific American Magazine, January 2006.

- Vijay Chandra. Dr., and Rajesh Pandav, Dr., **Mental Health and Psychosocial Support Activities in Response to The Tsunami Disaster in Maldives,** Detailed evaluation Impact Assessment and Recommendation for Disaster preparedness by world Health Organization.,South East Asia Regional office, Mental Health and Substance Abuse.

- Vivekanandan,V., **From the margins to centre stage – Consequences of Tsunami 2004 for the fisher folk of Tamil Nadu,** Presented to the Planning Commission, New Delhi, 2005.

- www.eeri.or

- www.indianexpress.org
- www.indiatoday.org
- www.kanyakumaritsunami.co.in
- www.thehindu.org
- www.tngovt.nic.org
- www.tsunami.com
- www.tsunami.in.
- http://www.developments.org.uk/articles/india-after-the-tsunami/
- http://www.odihpn.org/report.asp?id=2798
- http://www.kanyakumari.tn.nic.in/coastal.htm
- http://www.tn.gov.in/tsunami/tsunami-relief.html#Housing
- http://www.helpinghandonline.org/Tsunami_india_c_report.htm
- http://www.stephentrust.org/Stephens_Trust_Life_of_Fishermen.html

Index